FACTS AT YOUR FINGERTIPS

THE WORLD OF ENDANGERED ANIMALS

EUROPE

BROWN BEAR BOOKS

Published by Brown Bear Books Limited

4877 N. Circulo Bujia
Tucson, AZ 85718
USA

and

First Floor
9-17 St. Albans Place
London N1 ONX
UK

Library of Congress Cataloging-in-Publication Data available upon request.

ISBN-13 978-1-78121-076-5

In this book you will see the following key at top left of each entry. The key shows the level of threat faced by each animal, as judged by the International Union for the Conservation of Nature (IUCN).

EX	Extinct
EW	Extinct in the Wild
CR	Critically Endangered
EN	Endangered
VU	Vulnerable
NT	Near Threatened
LC	Least Concern
O	Other (this includes Data Deficient [DD] and Not Evaluated [NE])

For a few animals that have not been evaluated since 2001, the old status of Lower Risk still applies and this is shown by the letters **LR** on the key.

For more information on Categories of Threat, see pp. 54–57.

Editorial Director: Lindsey Lowe
Editor: Tim Harris
Design Manager: Keith Davis
Designer: Lynne Lennon
Children's Publisher: Anne O'Daly
Production Director: Alastair Gourlay

Printed in the United States of America

062014
AG/5534

CONTENTS

Habitats, Threats, and Conservation

Europe is a relatively small continent, stretching from the Atlantic coasts of Portugal, Spain, France, Ireland, and Norway in the west to Russia's Ural Mountains in the east—and from the Mediterranean Sea in the south to the Arctic Ocean. Unlike South America, Africa, Asia, and Australia, no part of the continent is in the tropics. Apart from one small area in the south of Spain, there are no true deserts. Nor are there any tropical rain forests.

Europe was the first continent where wholesale logging of forests took place, so many declines in animal populations must have occurred long before people took much notice of such things. What we do know is that in the United Kingdom the last brown bears were seen around 1000 CE, gray wolves became extinct in the 14th century, and Eurasian beavers suffered a similar fate two centuries later. For these large forest-dwelling mammals, a combination of forest clearance and hunting for meat, fur, or skins sealed their fate. Bears and wolves were also persecuted because they were a threat to people and their livestock. These animals now face less persecution and in many less densely populated areas they are experiencing a revival of their fortunes.

Varied Habitats

Along the north coast of the Mediterranean Sea, shores and coastal lagoons have been very important environments for large numbers of breeding and feeding herons, shorebirds, gulls, terns, and seals. For example, the Mediterranean monk seal is now considered to be Critically Endangered, with a total population of only 350-450. It has suffered from accidental human disturbance and deliberate persecution by some fishermen; also, many animals have been caught accidentally in fishing nets. These problems have cut numbers dramatically and this seal is at risk of extinction. Ports, vacation resorts, and golf courses are concentrated along the coastal strip in Portugal, Spain, France, Italy, and Greece. Beaches are more disturbed, inshore waters have

been polluted, and coastal lagoons have been drained for construction or to provide water for irrigation projects. The Tablas de Daimiel National Park in southern Spain was once of international importance for its birds, but was almost destroyed by an irrigation scheme in the 1970s; wildfowl stopped visiting because it no longer contained enough water. Much rocky chaparral, which was not considered good enough for agriculture, was turned over to housing schemes. There are, however, many protected areas along the Mediterranean coast. In Spain, for example, the Ebro Delta National Park protects the world's largest breeding colony of Audouin's gulls (classified as Near Threatened) as well as many other species of birds, amphibians, fish, and invertebrates.

Mountains and Plains

The mountain ranges of the Alps (France, Italy, Switzerland, and Austria), Pyrenees (Spain and France), and Dinaric Alps (Slovenia and Croatia) are cloaked in forest at lower altitudes, with grassy meadows above the tree-line. The Pyrenees have small populations of brown bears and birds of prey called lammergeiers, but sadly the Pyrenean ibex went extinct in 2000. The Alps have a great diversity of animal life, including gray

wolves, brown bears, lynx, chamoix, ibex, and marmots. Some species are found nowhere else, for example the Alpine field mouse and Bavarian vole. One species, the Alpine salamander, was discovered as recently as 1988 and is one of the world's rarest amphibians. Even within mountains there are important habitats for animals. Cave systems provide places for bats to hibernate in winter and roost during the summer. The limestone caves in the mountains of Slovenia and Croatia are important, too, for the world's only population of the olm, a blind amphibian that is now considered

Where once *there was scrubby chaparral, teeming with wildlife, much of the Spanish coastal strip has witnessed the large-scale development of roads, vacation apartments, and golf courses.*

Vulnerable. This animal is dependent on clean; fresh water. Even though the olm is protected, chemical-rich run-off from farms poses a threat.

In some areas of Spain, the *dehesa* is an unusual habitat of undulating oak parkland, with the ground between the trees being alternately grazed and cultivated. This environment provides food and breeding sites for azure-winged magpies, golden orioles, great spotted cuckoos, shrikes, and hoopoes, while thousands of common cranes fly south in fall to feast on the acorns. This is also where the last Spanish imperial eagles live. This magnificent bird of prey is classified as Vulnerable since its world population numbers just 450–600 birds.

Rolling grasslands, such as those found on the plains of Spain, Hungary, and Ukraine, are hot and dry in summer but often cold and wet in winter. Spanish ibex and Spanish imperial eagles live in Extremadura, Spain, as do large numbers of sandgrouse and bustards. In Hungary (where the grasslands are called *pusztas*) there are Endangered saker falcons, and in Ukraine the steppes have many wheatears and larks.

Forests and Wetlands

Although nowhere near as extensive as they once were, large areas of temperate broadleaved forest stretch across Europe, some of it very old. Bialowieza Forest, in Poland and Belarus, is a good example. Much of the forest has been protected since 1923 because it supports the last herds of European bison. Despite experiencing great destruction in both World Wars, this forest wilderness supports populations of brown bear, gray wolf, Eurasian lynx, Eurasian red squirrel, wild boar, moose, deer, and birds such as hazel grouse, three-toed woodpecker, and spotted nutcracker. This forest type is also rich in invertebrates, ranging from beetles to butterflies and moths.

Where drainage is poor on the floodplains of large rivers, there are lakes and marshes. While many of these wetland areas have been drained to meet the needs of agriculture, some important ones remain, including the Biebzra Marshes, in Poland, where Endangered aquatic warblers still breed, along with great snipe and Eurasian beavers. Farther west, in France, La Brenne is another important wetland—an important wintering ground for white-tailed eagles and a stopover site for many migrant birds in transit between northern Europe and Africa.

A wide band of coniferous forest—the taiga— stretches from Scandinavia through Russia and into Asia. Lynx, pine marten, polecat, brown bear, gray wolf, and flying squirrel are some of the well-known mammals of this region. Eurasian beavers build their lodges and dams across streams; they are known as "keystone" species because they create habitats for other animals. Forest clearings attract nesting cranes, sandpipers, and black grouse, while the densest areas of forest provide food for other birds, including crossbills, nutcrackers, capercailies, and hazel grouse. This is one of the least-threatened environments, but logging and clearance for development have nonetheless reduced its area.

In the far north, conifers are replaced by birch and willow scrub, with ptarmigan, bluethroats, and Lapland buntings. This scrub is, in turn, replaced by treeless tundra, completely inhospitable to all but the hardiest animals in winter but supporting massive numbers of breeding wildfowl and shorebirds in summer, taking advantage of billions of invertebrates on which to feed. Global warming will gradually melt the frozen ground, or permafrost, beneath the tundra, damaging it. Some bird species will decline as a result.

Beyond the tundra is the Arctic Ocean, whose surface freezes during winter. Again, global warming will change the nature of this. Despite the international ban on hunting whales, illegal hunting of these magnificent mammals does still take place off the north coast of Norway and Russia. Much of the coast of the Arctic Ocean is gently sloping, but near-vertical sea-cliffs provide a very different kind of coastline in northwest Europe. Ledges on these rocky cliffs make ideal places for millions of seabirds to lay their eggs. Murres, dovekies, razorbills, shags, and gannets all use this specialized habitat, while burrows in grassy slopes above the cliffs are used by Atlantic puffins and Manx shearwaters. The rocky intertidal zone at the base of the cliffs is usually rich in aquatic invertebrates, especially those that anchor themselves to the rocks. In recent years marine preserves have been established to protect these environments.

European tundra *is an environment of low plants and lichen-covered rocks, with some stunted trees. Barren in winter, it supports many endangered animals during the summer months.*

Eurasian Beaver

Castor fiber

Easy to catch and traditionally of high commercial value, the Eurasian beaver has been heavily hunted in the past. Today threats include habitat loss and water pollution, but reintroductions are taking place, and the species has been restored to a wide area of Europe.

Beaver furs are warm and make good clothes. Beaver meat is also edible, and the animals produce an oily scent called castoreum that was once widely prized as a traditional medicine. Beavers are, in fact, so useful to people that for centuries they were hunted and trapped in large numbers and, as a result, were driven to extinction over much of Europe. In Britain, for example, the last animals were killed before the start of the 16th century. By the early 20th century the world population of the Eurasian species had fallen to about 1,500 animals, dispersed across five main sites, with a few more in Siberia and western China.

The demise of the Eurasian beaver has now been halted by effective protection measures, and the species' fortunes have been revived by many successful reintroduction projects. So far, beavers have been restored to 13 European countries, including Latvia, the Netherlands, France, and Hungary, all of which now have thriving new beaver populations. Sweden has imported some animals from Norway, while others have been released in Lapland, although their chances of survival so far north are precarious.

There are now about 650,000 Eurasian beavers altogether, mostly in Europe, although a few can be found in Central Asia. Some even live in semiurban areas: There is a colony along a riverbank below the flight path into Geneva Airport. After asking the public for their views, a trial release was organized in Knapdale, Scotland, where 16 beavers were released into the wild in 2009—and seem to be thriving.

Shaping the Environment

Eurasian beavers live in small colonies of closely related animals. Although they sometimes use log piles for their dens, they do not build dams like their North American cousins, preferring instead to dig burrows. Nevertheless, each fall they gnaw and fell trees, setting up stores of twigs and leaves for the winter, an activity that has a major effect on their environment. In summer they feed on aquatic plants more than bark, but can still cause damage to trees and sometimes to crops as well.

Although some of the beaver's habits can be destructive to the

---

DATA PANEL

Eurasian beaver

Castor fiber

Family: Castoridae

World population: About 650,000

Distribution: Widespread (although patchy) from France to China; Mediterranean countries north to Scandinavia

Habitat: Broad river valleys, swamps, and floodplains where trees are found beside slow-flowing water

Size: Length head/body: 30–36 in (75–90 cm); tail: 11–16 in (28–38 cm). Weight: up to 84 lb (38 kg)

Form: Heavy body with dark fur and a broad, flattened tail. Large orange incisor teeth; small ears and eyes set near the top of the head

Diet: Plant material: mostly grasses, leaves, and twigs; over 300 different species have been recorded

Breeding: One litter per year of up to 8 young (usually 4–5); mature at just under 2 years. Life span 10 years in wild; up to 25 or more in captivity

Related endangered species: No close relatives that are endangered

Status: IUCN LC

environment, the same activities actually assist the survival of other animals. By felling trees beavers create open clearings, stimulating new growth that provides an ideal environment for warblers, insects, and shy mammals that find it difficult to live in unmodified forest. The beaver's large burrows can cause flooding and bank destruction, but beavers also obstruct the water flow, which is helpful to some species. In good beaver habitat there may be one colony every 500 yards (450 m) along a riverbank; in poor conditions the gap between colonies may be over 3 miles (5 km).

New Hazards

Although Eurasian beavers are still killed in some countries, hunting is no longer a serious problem for the species. Today there is a new danger in the increasing volume of road traffic. The effects of road accidents can be particularly severe, often wiping out whole families as they move between isolated ponds. Youngsters also disperse away from their birth colony when they are about two years old, sometimes traveling over 60 miles (100 km) to find a new home. In much of modern Europe such journeys are almost impossible to make without crossing roads, and many young beavers are killed as a result.

There is also a new threat from detergent pollutants in the water, which may interfere with the vital insulation provided by the beaver's fur. A potential problem for the future is that the American beaver was introduced to Finland in 1937, before it was realised it was a different species. The two species do not interbreed, but they do compete with each other for food resources.

Beavers *are at risk from natural hazards such as getting trapped under the ice in winter. Natural predators like wolves do them little harm. A greater danger is posed by highway traffic.*

Eurasian Red Squirrel

Sciurus vulgaris

Red squirrels are common across Europe, but are rapidly being replaced by American gray squirrels in Britain. Such a fate may also overtake their continental cousins.

Only 100 years ago the red squirrel was common and the only squirrel in Britain and across continental Europe. Now it is extinct in southern England, except on three islands off the coast. It remains common in Scottish forests and is still found in northern England, although its numbers there are declining fast. Apart from these areas, it survives in a few scattered localities in Wales and eastern and central England. In its place has come the American gray squirrel, introduced to Britain between 1876 and 1929. The American gray has proved a highly successful invader, becoming the squirrel commonly seen in most British woodlands, parks, gardens, and even in the middle of cities.

Many people blame the grays for attacking and driving out the native red squirrel or for passing on fatal diseases. In fact, there is no evidence that it is guilty of either of these crimes, although one natural disease that kills red squirrels does not affect grays. The main problem seems to be that while the European red squirrel is satisfactorily adapted to life in coniferous woodlands, it is simply less well equipped than the gray to survive in deciduous forests.

Gray squirrels originated in the hardwood forests of North America and are at home in similar woodland areas of lowland Britain. While the reds can survive in deciduous forests on their own, they are at a disadvantage in such environments when they face competition from the grays. The result is that once the grays spread into an area, the reds disappear within about 15 years. Attempts to reintroduce them back into the areas from which they disappeared have not been successful.

A Question of Adaptation

One major problem is that red squirrels cannot digest acorns properly. Acorns are the main food available in the fall in most lowland forests in Britain. Grays thrive on them, and they also compete for hazelnuts, the reds' favorite food in deciduous woodland. Since gray squirrels normally live at double the population densities of reds, they eat at least twice as many nuts, leaving the latter with insufficient food resources. Eurasian red squirrels feed mainly in the treetops, so they cannot afford to store much fat for the winter without running the risk of becoming clumsy

---

DATA PANEL

Eurasian red squirrel (European red squirrel)

Sciurus vulgaris

Family: Sciuridae

World population: Probably at least 2 million spread over a huge area

Distribution: Europe and Asia, from Britain east to China and northern Japan

Habitat: Forest, especially coniferous forest

Size: Length head/body: 7–10 in (18–24 cm); tail: 5–8 in (14–20 cm).

Weight: 9–12 oz (250–350 g)

Form: Bright chestnut red in summer, darker in winter; large bushy tail and (in winter) prominent ear tufts

Diet: Pine seeds, nuts, fruit, and fungi; occasionally insects and birds' eggs

Breeding: Usually 3 (but up to 8) young per litter; 1 or sometimes 2 litters per year after a gestation period of 5–6 weeks. Life span up to 7 years in the wild, but many die young; 10 years in captivity

Related endangered species: Some local populations and subspecies of squirrels and chipmunks in the U.S. are Critically Endangered, Endangered, or Vulnerable, but (as with the Eurasian red squirrel) whole species are not at risk

Status: IUCN LC

climbers. Grays, on the other hand, forage more on the ground and so can accumulate larger fat reserves because agility in the treetops is less important for them. With less fat to tide them over periods of scarcity, reds have to feed regularly, whatever the weather. Since they do most of their foraging in the trees, they are also limited in the range of food available to them. In contrast, the ground-feeding grays not only have access to a wider selection of forage but can also find enough to meet their needs in a much shorter time, a substantial advantage in spells of bad weather.

Ironically, native red squirrels have simply turned out to be less well adapted to cope with the British weather and living conditions than the invasive grays, and so they have lost out in competition with the newcomers. Red squirrels are now absent from most parts of England and many areas of Wales, although the population in Scotland (about 100,000 in 2008) seems much more secure.

The Eurasian red squirrel *spends much of its time foraging in trees; it comes down to the ground occasionally to bury nuts.*

Still more alarmingly, grays are now spreading across northern Italy. The species was introduced there in 1948 and in 1966, near Turin. If they spread, the grays will threaten red squirrels throughout the rest of Europe. Attempts to curb the threat to Eurasian red squirrels by eliminating the grays have been stopped by animal-rights supporters; in some places they have managed to win legal backing for their efforts to halt the killings.

The situation raises a difficult moral dilemma. If the few hundred introduced gray squirrels have a right to life, should the threatened red squirrel population not benefit from similar protection? And if so, how can their future be assured in the face of a challenge from outside, except by culling the newcomers?

European Souslik

Spermophilus citellus

Sousliks live in colonies underground. Their extensive tunnel systems are vulnerable to destruction by the modern agricultural machines that are replacing horse-drawn plows in eastern Europe.

Sousliks are the European equivalent of American prairie dogs. Both are ground squirrels that live in underground tunnel systems. While prairie dogs live in social groups called coteries that make up "towns" of interconnected burrows, sousliks live singly within colonies. Each animal has a separate burrow, usually with at least two entrances, but the burrows are close together and cover large areas of ground. The best souslik habitat has short, grassy turf growing over a deep, lime-rich soil that is easy to excavate. In some parts of Serbia, where the habitat is particularly suitable, souslik colonies support up to 20 animals per acre (48 per ha.)

Like prairie dogs, European sousliks sit upright at their burrow entrances, keeping watch for threats to their colony, especially from birds of prey cruising overhead. If danger is spotted, a souslik will let out a loud whistle to warn its neighbors. Foxes, cats, and dogs are also a threat, but rarely get close without being detected.

Sousliks like to eat fresh green vegetation, but they also pick up seeds and insects. They are normally active in the day and are vulnerable to predators out on the short grassland where they live. To reduce the dangers of feeding at the surface, they gather food quickly above ground and stuff it into their cheek pouches. They then scurry into their burrows to eat their meal in safety. Often the food is stowed away in special underground chambers.

Once the breeding season is over, usually by late June, the sousliks begin to build up their nutritional

DATA PANEL

European souslik (European ground squirrel)

Spermophilus citellus

Family: Sciuridae

World population: A few tens of thousands

Distribution: Southeastern Europe from Hungary to the Black Sea coast, but fragmented

Habitat: Open plains, fields, meadows up to 6,500 ft (2,200 m)

Size: Length head/body: 7.5–8.5 in (19–22 cm); tail: 2–3 in (5.5–7.5 cm). Weight: 8.4–10 oz (240–340 g)

Form: Squirrel with mottled brown fur, short tail, large eyes, and small ears

Diet: Fresh plant material gathered above ground; also seeds, insects, and roots

Breeding: One litter of 5–8 young per year, born April–June after gestation period of 3–6 weeks. Life span up to about 5 years

Related endangered species: Idaho ground squirrel *(Spermophilus brunneus)* EN; Mohave ground squirrel *(S. mohavensis)* VU; European spotted souslik *(S. suslicus)* NT; Washington ground squirrel *(S. washingtoni)* NT

Status: IUCN VU

reserves for winter. Large amounts of fat accumulate under the skin and around the intestines. The fat provides a store of energy to keep the animal alive while it is dormant. They start to hibernate in October, remaining cold and inactive underground until March. Hibernation enables them to escape the intense cold of continental winters and also helps them avoid the problem of seasonal food shortages as the plants die back during the winter months. Yet it also makes the animals vulnerable, since any form of disturbance can cause them to wake up. Emergence from torpor consumes energy reserves at about 10 times the rate used when staying in hibernation. Animals that are unable to fatten up sufficiently before hibernation and are woken in midwinter may end up starving to death.

Threats from Modern Farming

Sousliks are facing a problem like that confronting prairie dogs and mole-rats: changing farming methods. The switch from horse-drawn plows to tractors in eastern Europe has had a significant impact on the species. It has reduced the need for horses, so there is now much less land set aside on farms for grazing. Grass that would once have been cropped by the horses is left to grow tall and is cut for hay. Tall grass is an unsuitable habitat for sousliks.

Worse still, much former grazing land is now being plowed and used for growing arable crops, again an unsuitable environment for the animals. While the traditional horse-drawn plows only scraped the surface of the soil, powerful modern tractors pull implements that dig deep into the earth over extensive areas, destroying souslik colonies in the subsoil—a particular danger if cultivation takes place in early spring, while the animals are still hibernating. Heavy tractors also crush the burrows.

Already sousliks have become extinct in many parts of the central European plain, including Germany and Croatia. Since the agricultural nations of eastern Europe joined the European Union, and benefited from increased prosperity and investment in more efficient farming methods, the sousliks have been driven out of even more of their strongholds.

The European souslik *spends much of its time sitting upright on its haunches and keeping watch for predators such as foxes and birds of prey. Sousliks generally have large eyes and sharp eyesight.*

Greater Horseshoe Bat

Rhinolophus ferrumequinum

The greater horseshoe bat is vulnerable at every stage of its life cycle. Increasingly, the bats are under threat from destruction of their roosting sites and their food supply. The problem of dwindling populations is compounded by their low breeding rates.

The greater horseshoe bat is a broad-winged, large-eared insectivorous bat. Its name derives from the shape of the fleshy growth around its nostrils, which is used to focus sound when it is hunting by echolocation. Echolocation is when the bats produce short, high-frequency pulses that reflect from objects. By listening to the echoes, the bats determine the location of obstacles and prey.

Greater horseshoe bats roost by day and forage by night, hunting for insects over fields and in deciduous woodland. Males and females usually roost separately, but both sexes come together during the winter to hibernate, hanging with their wings wrapped around their body instead of folded at their sides (as in other bats). This exposes more wing surface to the air, resulting in high moisture loss from the horseshoe bat's body. Water loss is best prevented by hibernating in humid places, so horseshoe bats seek out caves, cellars, and old mines, which offer the right combination of cool, moist conditions. The need for caves limits bat numbers and restricts their distribution to areas where such suitable hibernation sites can be found.

Although they are widely distributed, greater horseshoe bats are now regarded as seriously threatened or endangered in many areas. They have recently become extinct in Belgium and the Netherlands. In Britain numbers have declined by over 90 percent in 50 years, and serious losses have been reported in other places too.

Threats from Modern Farming

All the bats' needs (including hibernation sites) must be met within about 30 miles (50 km). The number of available sites has been badly affected by the tendency in farming toward huge fields, removal of woodlands, filling in of caves, and the destruction or conversion of old farm buildings.

Bat flight is an energetic activity, so bats need to find plenty of food within a short distance of their roost, particularly when mothers are rearing their young. Serious problems arise when feeding areas

DATA PANEL

Greater horseshoe bat

Rhinolophus ferrumequinum

Family: Rhinolophidae

World population: Low thousands

Distribution: Southern Palearctic: Europe, and Asia north of the Himalayas

Habitat: Open deciduous woodland and farmland; hibernates in caves

Size: Length: 2.4–2.8 in (6–7 cm); wingspan: 14–16 in (35–40 cm). Weight: 1.2 oz (30 g)

Form: Mouselike animal with membranous wings and large ears; cone-shaped nose leaf around the nostrils

Diet: Large insects, including beetles and moths

Breeding: Only 1 young born per year, usually in mid-July but sometimes earlier; may be delayed by bad weather until August. Life span more than 30 years possible

Related endangered species: Many other bat species, including Morris's bat (*Myotis morrisi*)

Status: IUCN LC

Greater horseshoe bats *get their name from the shape of the fleshy growth on their face (below). When roosting, they hang free like a furled umbrella or cling to rocks (far right).*

around their nursery roost are destroyed. Mothers have to fly farther to feed and so use more energy for the same return. Providing milk to feed their young (which at birth are about one-third of the mother's own weight) also demands great energy.

Threats to insects also affect the bats. The greater horseshoes need to eat many large-bodied insects, particularly moths, beetles, and dung flies. Beetles and moths live around pasture, but such places are increasingly being turned into crop fields. In modern farming cattle are usually kept in barns for longer periods, so less dung is available to insects. Furthermore, modern veterinary treatments given to cattle have reduced the numbers of flies feeding on their dung. The use of insecticides also reduces the numbers of insects available to the bats.

Other Threats

Bats often rely on the roofs of houses and farm buildings as roosting sites. During the 1970s and 1980s chemicals were widely used in Europe to protect roof timbers from wood-boring insects. The chemicals remain toxic to bats for up to 20 years, and bats that consumed insects contaminated by the chemicals were also at risk. They stored the minute amounts of poison from the insects in their body, and as the poison built up over time, it began to affect the bats' breeding success.

Climate is a problem across the northern limit of the bats' range. Bad weather reduces the feeding success of the animals. If the early summer is poor, most of that year's young may die. Bats produce only one young a year, so they cannot afford many bad seasons, especially in light of all the other threats to their habitat.

EX
EW
CR
EN
VU
NT
LC
O

Greater Mouse-Eared Bat

Myotis myotis

The greater mouse-eared bat is one of Europe's largest bats. Once found in large colonies, populations have now declined significantly, and the bat is extinct in parts of its range.

There are other bats that are more endangered than the greater mouse-eared. Even so, the decline of the greater mouse-eared species has been so drastic and spread over such a wide area that its future is in doubt. It is already extinct in parts of northern Europe. The first British colony was discovered in the 1950s, but died out within 10 years. Another colony was found in 1969, but was destroyed in 1974. A single male lived on until the mid-1980s, after which there were occasional sightings including one at a roost in 2012. The bat is known to migrate seasonally, sometimes covering between 50 and 100 miles (80 and 160 km), so it could in theory recolonize southern Britain, perhaps from France. Yet it is scarce in France too, and the colonies are small.

Elsewhere, too, populations have declined alarmingly. The bat has not been seen in Belgium since 1961, and several of the colonies that used to live in the Netherlands died out in the 1950s. A colony in southern Germany that numbered about 4,500 bats in 1961 had been reduced to barely a tenth of that number by 1976. Three other colonies in Germany used to produce over 100 young each year in the 1950s, but only 13 were born 10 years later. In eastern Germany colonies of 400 to 500 bats declined by 85 percent in 30 years. However, not all the population trends are down. In Austria, for example, it was estimated that there were 76,000 of this species in 1999 and that numbers were still increasing in 2006.

A Multitude of Threats

No single explanation accounts for the bat's widespread decline across Europe. The intensification of agriculture that has been harmful in Britain, for example, was not such a problem in Poland, since farming practices remained relatively unchanged until recent years. Fires and other forms of damage are known to hit the species hard, simply because of its habit of congregating in large numbers in buildings or caves. Timber-treatment chemicals have probably also affected breeding colonies that used the roofs of buildings. In addition, many bats may have been deliberately killed. Nursery sites and roosts have been sealed up to keep the bats from using churches, castles, and other large buildings. Mouse-eared bats hunt over open areas of pasture, park, and open woodland. Since they are big, they need

---

DATA PANEL

Greater mouse-eared bat

Myotis myotis

Family: Vespertilionidae

World population: Over 100,000

Distribution: Central and southern Europe south to Israel and Jordan and east to Belarus

Habitat: Open woodland, parkland, and old pasture; often roosts in caves

Size: Length head/body: 2.6–3.1 in (6.7–7.9 cm); tail: 1.8–2.4 in (4.5–6 cm); wingspan: 13.8–17.8 in (35–45 cm). Weight: 1–1.4 oz (28–40 g)

Form: Large, short-nosed bat with broad wings and long ears, the front edges of which are curved backward. Fur, nose, and ears gray-brown

Diet: Mostly beetles, but also grass-hoppers, spiders, and moths

Breeding: One young per year, born from June onward. Life span up to 22 years

Related endangered species: Guatemalan bat *(Myotis cobanensis)* CR; 6 other *Myotis* species are listed as Endangered, including the Indiana bat *(M. sodalis)* and the gray bat *(M. grisescens)* of North America; 18 *Myotis* species are listed as Vulnerable

Status: IUCN LC

more food than their smaller cousins. They feed mainly on beetles, and beetles have become scarce over much of their range as a result of changing land use, particularly the conversion of farms from grazing to arable land, reducing the available food resources.

Disturbed Hibernation

The bats also hibernate in caves, and these have been subjected to considerable disturbance since the 1950s with the increasing popularity of caving as a sport. Noise and the fumes from cavers' carbide lamps cause the hibernating bats to wake up. In doing so, they consume vital reserves of fat that they need to last them throughout the winter. Each arousal uses up more fat than several days of normal hibernation. If the bats are not very fat in the first place, due to the reduced availability of their favorite foods, the additional loss of stored fat can make the difference between survival and death.

As in other large bat species, greater mouse-eared bat females do not normally begin to breed until they are at least a year old, so many may die without ever breeding at all. Even when they do have young, only one offspring is born per year, so the population is unable to withstand heavy losses. Reasons for the bat's decline over its entire range are not fully understood. However, the species now has full legal protection in all the countries in which it still occurs. Many depleted colonies are also protected from disturbance. In recent years the population seems to have stabilized, and it can only be hoped that protective measures will in time enable a recovery to take place.

The greater mouse-eared bat
has large, distinctive ears. As with other bats, its fingers are elongated and joined by a flight membrane that extends down the side of its body.

Eurasian Otter

Lutra lutra

The otter has become extinct in many parts of Europe as a result of habitat loss. Now conservation projects are underway, and the remaining populations are recovering.

A widespread and successful species, the Eurasian otter is found on the banks of rivers and lakes across a huge area of Europe and Russia as far east as China and Japan. It can survive intensely cold winters and feeds on a wide variety of fish and other aquatic animals. In Scotland and parts of Scandinavia otters also live along the seacoast, adjusting their behavior to prey on crabs and mollusks.

For centuries the otter was hunted for sport and for its valuable fur, yet populations were fairly stable. In the 1960s and 1970s otter numbers suddenly dropped, particularly in Britain, but also in the Netherlands, Germany, and other parts of Europe. This was partly as a result of habitat destruction. Turning rivers into canals, engineering projects for flood prevention, and general disturbance (particularly from an increase in leisure fishing) all contributed to a reduction in otter numbers. But the prime culprit in the otters' decline was the increasing use of agricultural chemicals, particularly insecticides such as DDT, aldrin, and dieldrin.

Dangerous Chemicals

The use of artificial chemicals on crops and seeds reduces destruction by insects and thereby increases crop yields. However, the toxins take a long time to be eliminated from the environment. When it rains, chemicals are washed off farmland into streams and lakes, where they contaminate the plankton. Fish that feed on the plankton accumulate the toxic residues in their bodies. In turn, an otter eating the affected fish will undergo a buildup of toxic material in its fat and liver. Even if the poisons do not reach lethal levels, the otters might be rendered sterile, and in the 1960s and 1970s this process drove otters into serious decline. As older otters died, there were no young to replace them, and whole populations collapsed.

In countries where agriculture was less intensive, otter populations remained healthy, notably in Portugal, Ireland, Greece, and northern Russia. Otters living along coasts also largely escaped because

DATA PANEL

Eurasian otter

Lutra lutra

Family: Mustelidae

World population: Several tens of thousands

Distribution: Widespread across Europe as far east as China, but in small populations; locally extinct in parts of western Europe

Habitat: Riverbanks and coastal areas

Size: Length head/body: 24–36 in (60–90 cm); tail: 14–18.5 in (36–47 cm); females 10% smaller than males. Weight: males 13.5–37.5 lb (6–17 kg); females 13.5–26.5 lb (6–12 kg)

Form: Long, slim body with short legs, dark-brown coat, and long, tapering tail. Broad muzzle, small eyes and ears. Feet webbed

Diet: Mainly fish (especially eels), but also frogs and occasionally birds. Crayfish and mollusks where abundant

Breeding: Can breed in any month, litters of 2–3 young (up to 5) once a year, or born in alternate years; mature in second year. Life span 3–4 years; increases to 11 in captivity

Related endangered species: European mink (*Mustela lutreola*) CR; European wolverine (*Gulo gulo*) VU; giant otter (*Pteronura brasiliensis*) EN

Status: IUCN NT

they fed on prey that had not been contaminated by agricultural pollutants. The coastal population of Scotland is one of the most successful in western Europe. This group of otters has suffered heavy losses, however, from oil spills and accidents near coastal oil terminals or shipwrecks.

The most dangerous agricultural chemicals are no longer used in most countries, and otter numbers are beginning to increase, spreading back into places where they had died out. However, new threats loom. Acid rain affects many rivers in Europe, leading to a reduction in the numbers of aquatic invertebrates. This leads to fewer fish and less food for the otters. Meanwhile, PCBs—chemicals from industrial sources—pollute many rivers. These accumulate like DDT, but they damage animals at much lower concentrations.

Eurasian otters *have smooth fur and a streamlined body. Populations are recovering, especially in Finland and in Britain, assisted by reintroductions from captive-bred stock.*

European Bison

Bison bonasus

Bison used to occur widely in the forests of Europe, but by the 19th century human encroachment on its habitat and poaching had brought the species to the brink of extinction. However, many captive herds now exist, and bison have been released back into the wild in several places.

The European bison is Europe's largest land mammal. It lives in small herds of about 20, favoring forests with old conifer trees, where it can come out to feed in grassy clearings. Bison are slow-moving animals, often spending over half their time resting. They need to drink almost every day, and this means that they often congregate in places close to water. Bulls live in separate herds from the cows when there are young around, but normally both sexes mix together, with the bulls often traveling between herds. The animals wander over more than 12,000 acres (5,000 ha), frequently overlapping with areas used by other bison groups.

Over time, as the human population of Europe increased and developed, numbers of bison shrank, and this species was in steady decline for over 1,000 years. By the 19th century only two populations remained. The herd in the ancient Royal Bialowieza

DATA PANEL

European bison

Bison bonasus

Family: Bovidae

World population: About 4,200 (2,700 free-ranging and 1,500 captive)

Distribution: About 200 enclosed groups and 32 wild populations in eastern Europe

Habitat: Forest edges near clearings

Size: Length: up to 10 ft (3 m); height at shoulder: up to 6.5 ft (1.9 m); males larger than females. Weight: 1,750–2,200 lb (800–1,000 kg)

Form: A large, stocky mammal bigger than an ox, with a short, thick, hairy neck, humped shoulders, and large head; small hind limbs. Head is held high, unlike the American species. It has a dark-brown hide, and there is a small mat of curly hair on top of the head and a small beard under the chin. Both sexes have horns

Diet: Bison spend about 95% of their feeding time eating grass, but also occasionally browse leaves and bark. In winter the animals are given additional hay to help them survive. They eat about 65 lb (30 kg) per day

Breeding: Breeding season August–October. Single calf born after 9-month gestation. Most calves born May–July and weaned at about 1 year; mature at 3–4 years. Life span more than 25 years

Related endangered species: American bison (*Bison bison*) NT

Status: IUCN VU

Forest of eastern Poland was protected and fed during the winter. However, after the forest came under Russian control, numbers declined due to poaching. In 1915 there were still 785 animals there, but the herd was wiped out during World War I, mostly shot for food. The second group, the Caucasus bison herd, became extinct in 1927, also due to poaching. About 50 individuals survived, scattered in parks and zoos in Sweden, Germany, and Poland. The modern population of bison has been bred from just 12 members of this herd, and starting in the 1950s, animals were released into several protected areas.

Revival of the Species

Today the most famous herd is that in the Bialowieza National Park. In 2012 this herd contained 450 animals and was one of four populations in Poland.

Six populations have also been reestablished in the Caucasus, numbering about 500 individuals. The total population is now more than 4,200, with 2,700 living in the wild and the rest in parks and zoos around the world. Two herds were established in Denmark in 2012 and a small herd of eight was released into the wild in Germany in 2013.

Although the European bison has been saved from extinction, it remains threatened by disease. Descended from only a small gene pool, the population is affected by inbreeding, leading to reduced survival rates among newborns. A lack of natural predators means that herds have to be culled to prevent competition for food and to remove the least fit animals.

The European bison *was saved from total extinction by effective conservation management.*

Orca

Orcinus orca

Orcas—or killer whales as they are more emotively known—are not man-eaters by nature. In the vast majority of encounters with humans it has been the people that have done the killing.

Orcas are the world's largest predators of mammals and birds. They are known to hunt seabirds, seals, sea lions, and also other whales and dolphins, including large baleen whales. The bulk of their food, however, is made up of much smaller fish and squid.

Orcas have never been a principal catch for whalers, but whaling crews whose main target was the larger baleen whales would also take orcas if they happened to come across them. Hunting reached a peak during the winter of 1979 to 1980, when whalers from the former Soviet Union alone killed more than 900 orcas in the Southern Ocean.

Orcas and fishermen have always competed for similar fish, such as salmon and cod. At times humans have benefited from the whales' efforts: Fishermen would sometimes drop nets to scoop up the dense shoals of fish rounded up by killer whales. More frequently, however, the rewards have gone the other way. Orcas have been known to leap in and out of purse seine nets (large nets used to enclose a school of fish) to steal the contents. They can also swim alongside drift nets (nets supported by floats or a drifter), biting off the body of every trapped fish and leaving irate fishermen to haul up nets full of heads. An orca eats between 2.5 and 5 percent of its body weight each day, a quantity of fish that some fisheries are simply not willing to give up. As a result, orcas have sometimes been killed in order to protect

DATA PANEL

Orca (killer whale)

Orcinus orca

Family: Delphinidae

World population: At least 50,000

Distribution: Worldwide

Habitat: Seas and oceans; generally in deep water, but most often seen close to shore

Size: Length: 18–33 ft (5.5–10 m); males can be almost twice as long as females. Weight: 3–10 tons (2.5–9 tonnes)

Form: Robust, jet-black body, with bright white chin, belly, and eye patch; gray saddle; dorsal fin tall, especially in males; pectoral fins large and paddle shaped

Diet: Fish, squid, seals, sea lions, turtles, and seabirds; also small whales and dolphins

Breeding: Single young born at any time of year after 17-month gestation; weaned at 14–18 months; mature at 12–16 years. Males may live up to 60 years, females to 90 years

Related endangered species: Hector's dolphin (*Cephalorhynchus hectori*) EN; pantropical spotted dolphin (*Stenella attenuata*) LC; striped dolphin (*S. coeruleoalba*) LC

Status: IUCN DD

fish stocks. One controversial incident took place in the mid-1950s, when the United States Navy, acting at the request of the Icelandic government, allegedly used machine guns to wipe out hundreds of orcas from selected fishing areas.

Orcas on Display

Several hundred killer whales have been captured alive and taken to marine parks and dolphinaria, where they are trained to perform a variety of tricks. Unpopular though the exploitation of captive whales is now, there is little doubt that such exhibitions have worked wonders for the killer whale's image, revealing its unexpectedly playful nature. The species has grown in public affection, causing many to question the morality of hunting orcas or indeed of keeping them in captivity.

One whale, a male called Keiko, came to symbolize the whole issue of cetaceans in captivity. A starring role in the feature film *Free Willy* made the Icelandic killer whale Keiko world-famous; and when news of his poor treatment in captivity reached the media, there were widespread calls for his rehabilitation and release. The process was a lengthy one. There were fears that a whale that had been captive for years could not survive in the wild. Keiko was eventually returned to a large sea pen in Iceland to help him acclimatize, and then to a Norwegian fjord where he died in 2003, aged 27.

Even when not subjected to direct persecution, killer whales are at risk. Being at the top of the marine food chain means that they are exposed to heavy accumulations of chemical contaminants in the flesh of their prey. Pesticides, fertilizers, sewage, and industrial effluents contain potentially harmful compounds, although no one yet knows just how damaging they might be.

Individual orcas *can be recognized from differences in the shape of the dorsal fin and the whales' black-and-white pattern.*

EX
EW
CR
EN
VU
NT
LC
O

Fin Whale

Balaenoptera physalus

Decades of overhunting decimated populations of the world's second-largest whale. Although protected now, the species is not recovering as well as predicted.

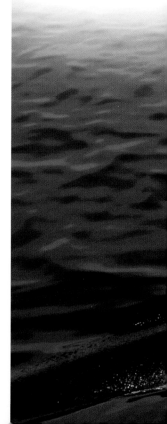

The fin whale is a near relative of the blue whale and comes a close second to its cousin in length, although it is not nearly as heavy as the blue. In other respects the two species are remarkably similar; hybrid fin-blue whales have even been identified by DNA analysis, much to the surprise of scientists. It may be that the two species have started interbreeding because of the scarcity of mates of the same species.

Fin whales are generally creatures of the open ocean and are rarely seen close to shore. They are also among the fastest-swimming whales and as a result were not widely hunted until the invention of steam-powered ships in the 1860s. The first commercial fin whale hunters were Norwegians, who began hunting in the North Atlantic. In 1868 the invention of the exploding harpoon made it much easier and less dangerous to kill large whales. Even so, the rate of killing in the North Atlantic was relatively low—at least by later standards—since each whale that was caught had to be tied to the side of the ship before it could be brought back to shore to be butchered.

Fatal Discovery

The real decline of the fin whale began after the discovery of vast herds of large whales that gathered each summer in the Southern Ocean. At the start of the 20th century the herds included up to a quarter of a million blue whales and well over half a million fin whales—about four-fifths of the world population. In the 1920s the invention of factory ships with ramps for loading whale carcasses on board meant that it was no longer necessary to bring every whale ashore.

The ships stayed at sea for weeks or months on end, processing the meat, oil, bones, and baleen of whale after whale. To begin with, the fin whale was not the target of choice for most whalers; but as the population of blue whales dwindled in the 1930s, more fin whales were taken. Apart from a brief respite during World War II, the catch increased steadily, reaching a peak of about 30,000 a year between 1952 and 1962.

By 1960 the southern population had fallen to just over 100,000. Despite the dramatic decline it was not until the late 1960s that the International Whaling Commission (IWC) succeeded in significantly reducing the kill. Eventually, in 1986 the IWC established a complete ban on the killing of fin whales for commercial purposes. By that time, however, there were fewer than 15,000 individuals remaining in the whole of the Southern Hemisphere.

Although a few countries persist in killing a number of fin whales each year for "scientific purposes," the species is now fairly well protected. However, in the 30 years since the decline of the fin whaling industry, the southern population of fin whales has not recovered as well as had been hoped. The main problem is that the teeming swarms of krill on which the whales feed are themselves being depleted by humans and by animals such as squid, seals, penguins, and various seabirds. These species increased in number as the whales declined, and now the ocean simply cannot support the number of whales it once did.

The fin whale faces other problems, too. Chemical contamination, loud noise, and global warming are altering the nature of its habitat. The fortunes of the fin whale, as of other species, are inextricably linked to the health of the oceans as a whole.

Fin whales *are migratory; both northern and southern populations spend their summers feeding in cold temperate and polar waters and migrate to warmer latitudes to breed in the winter. Yet individuals from the two populations never meet because the seasons in the different hemi-spheres are at opposite times of the year.*

DATA PANEL

Fin whale (finback, finner, herring whale, common rorqual, razorback)

Balaenoptera physalus

Family: Balaenidae

World population: About 100,000

Distribution: Three populations: in the North Atlantic, North Pacific, and Southern Ocean respectively

Habitat: Deep temperate and polar oceans

Size: Length: 59–73 ft (18–22 m), occasionally up to 86 ft (27 m); females about 10% bigger than males. Weight: 33–88 tons (30–80 tonnes)

Form: Long, slim-bodied whale with pointed snout; skin smooth and gray-black; right side of head white, left side dark; prominent dorsal fin placed well back on body

Diet: Fish, krill, and other crustaceans

Breeding: Up to 6 fetuses develop at once but only 1 young is success-fully reared; born after gestation of 11–11.5 months; weaned at 6–7 months; mature at 6–11 years. May live more than 100 years

Related endangered species: Blue whale *(Balaenoptera musculus)* EN; sei whale *(B. borealis)* EN; minke whale *(B. acutorostrata)* LC

Status: IUCN EN

Minke Whale

Balaenoptera acutorostrata

Saved by a worldwide ban on whaling in the 1980s, the minke whale is more numerous than its larger cousins. However, if some nations were to resume commercial whaling, the minke would be top of their list to hunt.

D espite being the smallest of the rorqual (filter-feeding whalebone) whales, the average minke weighs in at 9 tons (8 tonnes). A large proportion of its bulk is meat and blubber, products for which it has been hunted on a small scale for hundreds of years. Until relatively recently minkes had escaped the wholesale slaughter that nearly wiped out their larger cousins. For several decades the overexploitation of blue and fin whales in the Southern Ocean actually benefited the minke, because it reduced the amount of competition for food.

The minke whale *has a thick layer of blubber that enables it to venture farther into the icy waters of the Arctic and Antarctic than any of its close relatives. Minkes eat enough during the summer to last them through the winter, when they migrate to warmer waters and do not feed.*

In large whales the time at which an individual reaches sexual maturity is determined more by size than age. When food is plentiful—as it was for southern minkes between the 1950s and 1970s—young whales grow much faster and mature more quickly. In 1944 an average minke first bred at about 13 years of age. By the early 1980s most minkes were sexually mature after only six years. Not surprisingly, the population boomed, increasing by 800 percent in the period from 1930 to 1979.

Commercial Whaling

By the early 1970s factory whaling ships had all but wiped out the largest species of rorqual whale and had begun to hunt minkes. Although much smaller than blue and fin whales, and so less valuable, minkes were by that time far more numerous and much easier to catch. Minkes are more curious than other large whales and readily approach ships. Many paid dearly for their curiosity: The minke death toll peaked at over 12,000 a year by 1977. At this time the scale of the slaughter prompted growing public outrage. The

DATA PANEL

Minke whale

Balaenoptera acutorostrata

Family: Balaenopteridae

World population: 182,000 (2000 estimate)

Distribution: Global

Habitat: Deep water, but seldom more than 100 miles (160 km) from land

Size: Length: 26–36 ft (8–11 m); female slightly larger than male. Weight: 7–11 tons (6–10 tonnes)

Form: Slim whale with markedly triangular head; skin dark gray above, fading to almost white on belly; often has pale chevron-shaped patch around pectoral fin

Diet: Antarctic populations eat mostly krill (planktonic shrimp); northern minkes also consume squid and small fish

Breeding: Single calf born after gestation of 10–11 months; weaned at 5 months; mature at 6 years. Life span up to 60 years

Related endangered species: Blue whale (*Balaenoptera musculus*) EN; fin whale (*B. physalus*) EN; sei whale (*B. borealis*) EN

Status: IUCN LC

minkes were saved by the international ban on whaling that was put in place in 1986. To begin with, Japan and Norway ignored the ban, protesting that minkes were not endangered. However, the fact that minke whales were protected before the species reached crisis point is the main reason that they are relatively secure today.

About 1,000 minke whales are still killed each year; some as part of legal traditional hunts by indigenous peoples, others for "scientific" purposes. International regulations allow a number of whales to be killed each year for research, a loophole that has been exploited by some whaling nations, principally Japan. There is no doubt that the market for whale parts is alive and well, and meat from the "scientific" quota of minke whales often ends up on sale to the Japanese public. The northwestern Pacific population

of minke whales is already the smallest, with just 25,000 individuals. There is little doubt in the minds of most conservationists that if commercial whaling were allowed to begin again, it would get out of hand, since it is difficult to enforce quotas.

Mini Minkes

Whaling is not the only subject of minke whale debate. For many years scientists have recognized the existence of a different type of minke living in the Southern Hemisphere. Known as dwarf minkes, the whales rarely grow longer than 23 feet (7 m) and have a distinctive white patch extending from the base of the pectoral fins onto the flank. Some scientists recognize the southern form as a separate species, but it may only be a local variety, and a full comparative study has yet to be made.

Northern Right Whale

Eubalaena glacialis

Even after almost 80 years of international protection, the northern right whale is battling extinction. Intensive conservation is needed to halt the damage inflicted by 1,000 years of unregulated hunting.

Northern right whales are the most endangered of all the large whales, and the species' name describes the main reason: For centuries the animal was known to whalers as the "right whale" to hunt. It lived close to the shore, fed near the surface, was easy to approach by boat, and floated when it was dead. Furthermore, a single carcass could yield several hundred barrels of oil—even more than the blue whale—and its long, thin baleen (whalebone) plates were considered to be of the finest quality.

European right whales were hunted to virtual extinction by the early 18th century. By then the American whaling industry was well established and had already depleted the western Atlantic stocks. In the mid-19th century American whalers could make $10,000 profit on a single carcass—equivalent to a third of a million dollars in today's terms. With such vast fortunes to be made, the whalers turned their attention to the right whales of the eastern North Pacific (since 2004 considered a separate species, North Pacific right whale, *Eubalaena japonica*). In the space of about 10 years these had become as rare as their Atlantic counterparts.

Death by Misadventure

Although northern right whales have been protected by international agreement since 1937, the population has barely increased, and many whales still die needlessly. Some fatalities result from boats accidentally plowing into whales feeding in busy shipping lanes. The true figure for these deaths is not known since shipping accidents often involve collisions with "unidentified submerged objects," and a wounded whale may travel some distance before dying alone and unrecorded. Whales are also often killed or injured in accidents involving fishing nets and tackle.

End of the Line

The average birthrate of right whales in the northeast Atlantic dropped from one young born per female every three years in the 1980s to one birth every five years a decade later. Pollution in European coastal waters may be one reason since the chemicals in industrial effluent are known to build up in the body tissues of whales, causing illness or death.

DATA PANEL

Northern right whale

Eubalaena glacialis

Family: Balaenidae

World population: North Atlantic: 300–350; North Pacific: a few hundreds

Distribution: Coastal regions of North Atlantic and North Pacific. Populations in North Atlantic and North Pacific now considered different species

Habitat: Temperate ocean

Size: Length: 40–55 ft (13.6–18 m); females slightly larger than males. Weight: 22–112 tons (20–102 tonnes)

Form: Large black whale with long, tapering body; no dorsal fin; huge mouth with arched upper jaw; head with barnacle-encrusted skin callouses

Diet: Planktonic crustaceans

Breeding: Single calf born every 2–5 years after 13-month gestation; season of birth varies with regions; weaned at 7 months; mature at 9 years. Life span unknown but probably at least 30 years

Related endangered species: Southern right whale (*Eubalaena australis*) LC

Status: IUCN EN

The decline in birth rate may be partly due to pollutants called endocrine disrupters, which interfere with normal bodily functions by blocking or mimicking the actions of hormones. Another explanation may be inbreeding due to the small size of the remaining populations, a theory borne out by the increased number of miscarriages and genetic abnormalities.

In recent years changing weather patterns in the North Atlantic have led to a decrease in the abundance of marine plankton, the whales' main food source. This may be temporary, but even if conditions revert to normal, it may be too late to save the species. There is evidence that competition between right whales and sei whales, which are also endangered, is increasing as the two species are forced to occupy similar niches and compete for a diminishing quantity of plankton.

The northern right whale *lacks a dorsal (back) fin and has barnacle-encrusted skin callouses on its head.*

At the current rate of decline the last northern right whale will probably die in about 190 years. The estimate is this long only because the whales are long-lived. The point of no return, when the remaining northern right whales no longer constitute a viable breeding population, may be reached much sooner.

Eurasian Bittern

Botaurus stellaris

This extremely secretive bird of lowland reed beds has declined over much of its European range as a result of the destruction of wetland habitat. It is hoped that new conservation initiatives to study the Eurasian bittern and preserve its habitat will help assure its future.

The Eurasian bittern, a large member of the heron family, has a very restricted habitat. During the breeding season it is found exclusively around areas of shallow, still, or slow-flowing fresh or brackish water fringed by extensive growth of reeds (or occasionally bulrushes or cattails). It hides among the reeds and sites its nest in swampy areas, away from predatory land mammals. The bittern requires water channels free from reeds but hidden from view in which to search unseen for food: mainly fish but also other animals.

The Eurasian bittern prefers areas with a mixture of old and young reeds, but outside the breeding season it is less exacting in its requirements and may occur in smaller reed beds, flooded grassland, overgrown ditches, cress beds, and rice paddies.

The Eurasian bittern's striped brown, golden-buff, and black plumage provides superb camouflage. When it senses danger, it stretches its body and neck vertically, pointing its bill skyward, so that its stripes blend perfectly with the tall reed stems. It can stay like this for several hours and completes the disguise by swaying gently to imitate the movement of the reeds in the breeze. At the same time, it swivels its eyes forward to keep a lookout for any intruder.

Bitterns spend almost all their time during spring and summer hidden from view among the reeds, making it impossible to assess numbers by direct observation. Estimates can be made listening for the characteristic booming song of the males. Individual males can be identified by their unique voiceprint. Depending on wind conditions, the repeated deep, resonant notes can be heard over 3 miles (5 km) away. Unfortunately, it is impossible to equate the number of booming males with breeding pairs, since each male may mate with up to five females.

Persecution and Habitat Destruction

Once common and widespread over most of the temperate parts of Europe, the Eurasian bittern has suffered both from large-scale drainage of wetlands and as a result of human persecution. It is still reasonably common in some countries, such as Russia, Poland, and Romania, but

DATA PANEL

Eurasian bittern (great bittern, bittern)

Botaurus stellaris

Family: Ardeidae

World population: 110,000–340,000. Russia and Ukraine hold major populations. In western Europe only Britain, France, and Netherlands have more than 100 booming males

Distribution: From western Europe and central Russia to the Pacific; a few small populations in southern Africa

Habitat: Extensive lowland reed beds; occasionally found in dense stands of cattail and bulrushes

Size: Length: 27.5–31.5 in (70–80 cm); wingspan: 4–4.4 ft (1.3–1.4 m). Weight: male 2.1–4.2 lb (1–1.9 kg), female 1.9–2.4 lb (0.9–1.1 kg)

Form: Large, thick-necked heron; brown and black striped plumage

Diet: Mainly fish, amphibians, and insects; also leeches, worms, mollusks, crustaceans, spiders, lizards, and small birds and mammals

Breeding: Five to 6 olive-brown eggs incubated for 3.5–4 weeks; young fledge at 7–8 weeks

Related endangered species: Eight heron species are threatened, including 1 other bittern: Australasian bittern *(Botaurus poiciloptilus)* EN

Status: IUCN LC

in most of central, western, and southern Europe it is in steep decline. In the British Isles of the 17th century, for instance, the species bred throughout most of England, Wales, Ireland, and southern parts of Scotland; but by the early 1800s its breeding range had dwindled to only a few sites, mainly in the southeast, where suitable large reed beds remained in the undrained fens and marshes.

As well as suffering from habitat destruction, the Eurasian bittern was highly regarded as food. In addition, its eggs were prized by collectors, and many birds were also shot for museum exhibits and for their feathers, which were used in the making of fishing flies. Severe winter weather also took its toll on bittern populations. The net result of all these factors was that by 1868 the bittern was effectively extinct as a breeding bird in the British Isles.

Hope for the Future
From 1911 the bittern began to recolonize Britain from the European mainland, breeding first in the Norfolk Broads in eastern England. A slow increase resulted in about 25 booming males by 1930. By 1954 the species had increased in both numbers and range, with an estimated total of between 78 and 83 booming males breeding regularly in seven counties. Then, from the late 1950s, the species suffered another decline across Europe.

Between 1970 and 1990 half of all European countries with breeding bitterns experienced population declines of over 50 percent. The reasons are complex, but they include water pollution, water overenrichment (often causing algal growth), die-back of reeds, and the abandonment of traditional wetland management, resulting in the invasion of scrub into previously reeded areas.

By 1997 the British population was at an all-time low and facing extinction once again, with only 11 booming males known. A major rescue program was launched during the 1990s involving several conservation organizations. Measures taken included a research project on the bittern's ecology, the establishment of new reserves, the planting of new reed beds—for example, in Somerset—and the enlargement and improvement of existing ones. As a result, there has been a modest but distinct increase in booming males: 13 in 1998, 19 in 1999, and 104 in 2011. The most dramatic increase has been on the Somerset Levels, where there has been a major initiative to improve the reed beds and where there were 25 males in 2011.

The Eurasian bittern's *striped plumage provides perfect camouflage in its dense reed-bed habitat.*

Lesser Kestrel

Falco naumanni

The lesser kestrel suffered big declines in the second half of the 20th century in its breeding range and still faces threats at its migratory stopover sites and on its wintering grounds in Africa. Changes in farming and the use of pesticides have affected insects—and the lesser kestrels that depend on them.

The good news is that in the early years of the 21st century there have been signs of a recovery in the fortunes of this falcon. As its common name suggests, the lesser kestrel is a smaller, more delicately proportioned relative of the common kestrel, one of the most abundant and successful of the world's birds of prey. Unlike the latter, the lesser kestrel has a patchy breeding distribution across Europe and in parts of North Africa and Asia, with concentrations of birds in suitable habitats and large gaps in between. Many birds spend the winter farther south in Africa.

The lesser kestrel experienced massive declines over most of its limited range in Europe between 1950 and 2000. In Spain, the species' European stronghold, more than 100,000 pairs are thought to have bred in the early 1960s. By 1994 numbers had declined to only 8,000 pairs (although the breeding population had risen to more than 12,000 pairs by 2010).

Unusually for a bird of prey, the lesser kestrel is extremely gregarious. It usually breeds, hunts for food, roosts, migrates, and winters in groups. Nesting colonies are mainly close to human settlements, and the birds prefer holes and ledges high in tall, old buildings. By nesting high up, they try to avoid climbing mammal predators, especially rats, which can seriously affect some populations. (In one Portuguese colony, for example, rats ate 39 percent of the eggs.)

The lesser kestrel is a summer visitor to almost its entire breeding range, migrating in the fall to spend winter mainly in the drier parts of Africa south of the Sahara. The birds probably cross the Mediterranean, the Sahara, and the Middle East in fast, high-altitude, nonstop flights of a minimum of 1,500 miles (2,400

km), those from Asia making much longer journeys. In spring the birds return to their breeding grounds. The males arrive first and immediately lay claim to nest sites. The species' southerly distribution reflects the importance of insects in its diet, especially large ones such as grasshoppers, locusts, crickets, beetles, and earwigs. Generally about 80 to 90 percent of its food consists of insects and smaller numbers of other invertebrates, including large, poisonous centipedes.

Disappearing Prey

Dramatic changes in farming have had a major effect on lesser kestrel populations. The advance of intensive agriculture has swept away many of the meadows, pastures, and steppelike habitats, making it hard for the birds to find enough insect food. Areas of uncultivated grassland and cereal crops have been widely replaced by fields of sunflowers; not only does the crop contain less suitable prey, but the increased height and density of the plants mean that kestrels take much longer to find and catch the insects. Abandonment of farmland has allowed scrub and trees to invade the open landscape—also bad for the birds.

The large-scale use of pesticides has also greatly reduced numbers of the lesser kestrel's insect prey. Renovation of old buildings has deprived other colonies of their nest sites. Land-use changes and heavy pesticide use in their African winter quarters have also taken their toll.

Lesser kestrel *breeding populations in Europe and North Africa declined by 95 percent between 1950 and 2000 before increasing to 25,000 pairs by 2010.*

DATA PANEL

Lesser kestrel

Falco naumanni

Family: Falconidae

World population: Estimated at more than 25,000 pairs

Distribution: Scattered breeding colonies across parts of southern Europe, North Africa, Turkey, Central Asia, southern Russia, eastern Mongolia, and northern China. Most birds move south in winter, including to southern Arabia and southern Africa

Habitat: Lowlands and foothills in Europe; up to 4,900 ft (1,500 m) in Asia. In open country, such as deserts, dry grassland, and low-intensity farmland

Size: Length: 11.5–12.5 in (29–32 cm)

Form: An elegant bird of prey with narrow, pointed wings and a long, slim tail, wedge-shaped at the tip; male much more colorful than barred-brown female, with gray-blue, rust-red, and whitish plumage pattern

Diet: Mainly insects; also some lizards, small mammals, and birds

Breeding: Usually 3–5 white to buff eggs with reddish spots or blotches, laid mid-April to May. Incubation 4 weeks; fledging 5–6 weeks

Related endangered species: Mauritius kestrel *(Falco punctatus)* VU; Seychelles kestrel *(F. araea)* VU; gray falcon *(F. hypoleucos)* VU; taita falcon *(F. fasciinucha)* NT; New Zealand falcon *(F. novaeseelandiae)* NT

Status: IUCN LC

Corncrake

Crex crex

Corncrakes are considerably more numerous than was thought a few years ago, but changes in agricultural practices are likely to trigger rapid population declines in the near future.

The corncrake occupies one of the largest ranges of any threatened species. It breeds from Ireland, Britain, France, and possibly Spain in western Europe east to Asiatic Russia, Mongolia, and China. The species migrates south in the nonbreeding season to the southern parts of sub-Saharan Africa, and birds have been recorded on migration in a large number of countries throughout Central Asia, northern Africa, and the Middle East.

The birds' numbers are exceptionally large for a threatened species. The total European population is estimated to be between 1.1 and 1.8 million singing males, with a further 0.5 to 1.2 million in Asia. Since corncrakes are generally elusive, the only effective method of surveying them is by listening for the far-carrying calls of the male. However, conservationists have not always known that the population was

so large. As recently as 1996 the best estimate was 92,000 to 233,000 singing males. The discrepancy in numbers raises two questions: Why have the estimates increased so dramatically in recent years, and why is such a widespread and numerous species still considered threatened?

The first question is the easier to answer. The recent upward revision of numbers results from improved surveying of the species and increased collaboration among conservationists. In 1996 the European Union and the Council of Europe endorsed an action plan that has led to a host of national action plans across the continent. In 1998 a Corncrake Conservation Team was established, bringing together researchers, ornithologists, and conservation organizations working across the species' great range. In addition, the species is covered by what is probably

DATA PANEL

Corncrake

Crex crex

Family: Rallidae

World population: Estimated at about 5 million birds, with numbers in Asia especially uncertain

Distribution: Breeds over a huge range in Europe and Asia; winters in sub-Saharan Africa

Habitat: Agricultural grassland managed for hay production in Europe; some wetlands and other grasslands and savannas in Africa

Size: Length: 10.5–12 in (27–30 cm); wingspan: 16.5–21 in (42–53 cm). Weight: male 4.5–7.5 oz (130–210 g); female 5–5.5 oz (138–158 g)

Form: Upperparts brown with black streaking; underparts pale brown with cinnamon barring on flanks. The reddish

wings and dangling legs in flight are obvious features. More often heard than seen; its repetitive, far-carrying, "crex-crex" cry is given mainly at night and in the early morning

Diet: In the breeding season a wide range of invertebrates; mostly seeds in the fall and winter

Breeding: Believed to be polygamous (has more than 1 mate), with some males moving far to new singing areas. Nest is built on ground in dense vegetation from dead stems and leaves. Average clutch size 10 eggs; possibly 2 broods per season

Related endangered species: Forty-five in the family Rallidae, including Zapata rail (*Cyanolimnas cerverai*) CR; snoring rail (*Aramidopsis palteni*) VU; austral rail (*Rallus antarcticus*) VU; and Inaccessible rail (*Atlantisia rogersi*) VU

Status: IUCN LC

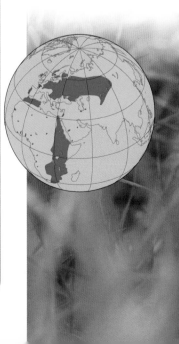

the most powerful international piece of legislation currently affecting threatened birds: the European Union's Wild Birds Directive. The combined efforts of people in many countries have resulted in improved reporting and conservation.

The Threat from Intensive Agriculture

The other question as to why the species is still considered threatened is altogether more complex. First, there is evidence of long-term decline in Europe. Between 1970 and the early 1990s 22 European countries, including those with the largest populations, such as Russia and Belarus, saw declines of between 20 and 50 percent. The falls were caused mainly by the intensification of agriculture, since throughout Europe the species primarily depends on grassland managed for hay production. The mechanization of hay and silage mowing and the practice of starting mowing earlier in the year are both significant threats, reducing nesting success and the survival rates of chicks and adults.

There are also concerns that such practices are extending to other parts of the corncrake's range. As land that was abandoned following privatization in eastern Europe and Russia becomes overgrown or is returned to intense management, numbers are likely to fall rapidly. Overgrown habitats will become too scrublike, while, as trends in western Europe have shown, the species is unable to adapt to intensive agricultural areas.

Improved habitat-management techniques have been investigated in response to the corncrake's threatened status; it is known, for example, that mowing fields from the center outward reduces the killing of chicks. The development and introduction of such strategies are the key to maintaining healthy corncrake populations in the future.

Across much of Eurasia *the corncrake is known for its repetitive rasping "crex-crex" cry, uttered by male birds in the springtime breeding season for hours on end.*

Great Bustard

Otis tarda

Despite its vast natural range across much of Europe and Asia, the magnificent great bustard is struggling to survive as its open steppe habitats are gradually transformed by the spread of intensive farming methods.

A male great bustard displaying in the spring breeding season is an astonishing sight. The huge, stately bird suddenly upends its tail and wings to reveal great fans of snow-white feathers, while inflating its throat pouch to erect a brush of gray plumage that almost conceals its head.

This sight was once commonplace on the open steppes that originally covered vast tracts of Europe and Asia. The rolling, almost treeless plains were ideal great bustard habitat, offering the largely flightless birds freedom of movement and a wealth of food.

Flocks of thousands pecked their way across the flower-rich grasslands, searching for shoots and seeds, grasshoppers, beetles, and the occasional lizard.

When people started felling the forests for farmland, the bustards took the opportunity to extend their range, learning to live and breed on the newly plowed land among the crops. In the 18th century there were probably more great bustards than ever before, and in Germany children were given time off from school to help chase the hungry flocks off the fields and collect their eggs for food.

Tempting Targets

A large, meaty animal, the great bustard has always been hunted. The invention of the shotgun made it vulnerable, and by the beginning of the 19th century the birds were being slaughtered in large numbers. Today, too, hunting remains a major problem; in Spain more than 2,000 bustards were killed every year before they received legal protection in 1980.

Yet the main threat to the bustard's survival is less obvious than hunting. Throughout the 19th and 20th centuries agriculture became steadily more intensive as farmers found new ways of feeding crops and destroying weeds and pests. Gradually, extensive, weed-strewn fields gave way to tightly controlled blocks of farmland separated by fences. This destroyed the open landscapes the birds require for successful breeding. In the 1970s the situation worsened with the widespread adoption of chemical pesticides that kill the weeds and insects the bustards eat.

DATA PANEL

Great bustard

Otis tarda

Family: Otididae

World population: 44,000–57,000

Distribution: Scattered over the grassy plains of Morocco, Portugal, Spain, central Europe, Turkey, Russia, southwestern and Central Asia, Mongolia, and China

Habitat: Steppe grassland, pasture, and lightly wooded areas; also farmland that is not intensive

Size: Length: 30–41 in (75–105 cm); wingspan: 6.2–8.5 ft (1.9–2.6 m). Weight: male up to 40 lb (18 kg); female up to 11 lb (5 kg)

Form: Large, upright, deep-chested, and robust bird with long legs and a long, thick neck. Barred black-and-gold upperparts, pale blue-gray head and neck, white underparts

Diet: Mainly young shoots, leaves, flowers, and seeds, plus insects and small vertebrates

Breeding: Male uses spectacular breeding display to attract and mate with as many females as possible. Mated females nest alone, laying 2–3 eggs in a depression on the ground in April–May. Eggs hatch in 3–4 weeks; young fledge at 4–5 weeks

Related endangered species: Great Indian bustard (*Ardeotis nigriceps*) VU; Houbara bustard (*Chlamydotis undulata*) VU; Bengal florican (*Houbaropsis bengalensis*) CR; lesser florican (*Sypheotides indica*) EN; little bustard (*Tetrax tetrax*) NT

Status: IUCN VU

The spectacular display *of the male great bustard is a reproductive tactic designed to attract the maximum number of mates during the breeding season.*

projects. In eastern Europe and Asia the outlook is bleak. In Europe the collapse of communism put much of the land in private ownership, and it looks much of this has become farmed intensively along Western lines. There are still 8,000–12,000 bustards in Russia, but in China and Mongolia intensive farming, grassland fires, and hunting have reduced populations to less than 5,000.

The main hope for the great bustard lies in the reversal of the trend toward intensive, chemical-based agriculture, coupled with specific measures such as the prevention of steppe fires and illegal hunting. Providing protected areas of habitat may also help; but since the birds need to roam over large areas, they do not thrive in enclosed wildlife reserves. Ultimately, their future will probably depend on persuading farmers to conserve their unique wildlife heritage. Since 2004 great bustards from Russia have been released on open grassland at Salisbury Plain in England, part of a program to reestablish the species there. Chicks have hatched, although they have been preyed on by foxes.

Plummeting Numbers

As a result, bustard numbers have crashed over the past few decades. In Hungary an estimated 8,500 in 1941 slumped to 3,400 in 1980 and shrank again to 1,100 by 1995. In Germany the 800 bustards counted in the 1970s had dwindled to 130 by 1993. In many other countries the situation is much the same. The only large, well-documented European population is in Spain, where between 29,000 and 34,000 great bustards—more than half the world total—still thrive on the dry grasslands. Yet even here their future is threatened by the cultivation of old pasture, building of fences, and installation of irrigation and drainage

Ibiza Wall Lizard

Podarcis pityusensis

The colorful appearance of this lizard has made it popular among hobbyists and consequently a frequent victim of illicit trade. It is also vulnerable to the effects of tourism on its environment.

Although the Ibiza wall lizard takes its name from Ibiza, one of the main islands in the Balearics, it is also found on numerous smaller islands, some of them little more than rocky islets with hardly any vegetation. It is quite adaptable, often found near human habitation in stone walls and ruined buildings, but also existing in scrubland and quite barren areas, even on steep cliffs.

The shape and coloration of the lizard vary from island to island. This variation has been a source of interest to scientists, and over 40 different subspecies of *Podarcis pityusensis* have been named. However, not all zoologists recognize these as subspecies. In some cases the situation has been confused by the construction of causeways linking islands. Fishermen have also collected particularly colorful lizards from one island and released them on another nearer home so that they can be collected and sold if the opportunity arises. This has led to some interbreeding between different "subspecies," making study difficult.

The Ibiza wall lizard is an attractive creature, and reptile-keeping hobbyists have been eager to add it to their collections. Collectors ranged from vacationers who took home a few specimens or reptile enthusiasts who took some for themselves and some to sell, to those operating on a commercial scale. Seizures by customs have included 2,000 lizards at Schipol Airport, the Netherlands, and two seizures of 500 and 400 lizards found packed in suitcases at Heathrow Airport, England. Out of the batch of 500 only 80 lizards survived their trauma to be flown back to the Balearic Islands. No doubt other batches have got through undetected. Under Spanish law collecting lizards is illegal, but the law is not always rigorously enforced.

The main source of income on the Balearic Islands used to be agriculture: Olive groves, grapes, almonds, and citrus fruit

DATA PANEL

Ibiza wall lizard

Podarcis pityusensis

Family: Lacertidae

World population: Unknown

Distribution: Balearic Islands, Spain

Habitat: Dry, rocky areas with some plant cover; sometimes found in stone walls and ruined buildings

Size: Length: varies from island to island, but on average 6–8 in (15–20 cm)

Form: Color and shape vary from island to island. "Large island" populations generally green on back, sometimes brown or gray, light lines along sides interspersed with spots or streaks; "small island" populations are sometimes melanistic—lack light pigments—tending to be black, dark brown, or dark blue, often with a dorsal pattern; some have blue or orange areas on flanks

Diet: Mainly insects, some small invertebrates; sometimes young geckos or their own young; occasionally fruit, berries, and nectar

Breeding: Possibly 2 clutches per year of 2–6 eggs

Related endangered species: Lilford's wall lizard (*Podarcis lilfordi*) EN; Milos wall lizard (*P. milensis*) VU

Status: IUCN NT

SPAIN

Majorca — Minorca

Ibiza — Balearic Islands

Formentera

ALGERIA

Lizard populations *in the Balearic Islands have evolved in isolation as rising waters of the Mediterranean Sea have cut off the islands from the mainland.*

were the main crops. The 1960s saw a rapid increase in tourism, which brought large amounts of money to the islands. The warm climate, sandy beaches, and attractive scenery continue to draw thousands of tourists every year. Tourism now accounts for 80 percent of the islands' income; many local people now work in the tourism industry.

Habitats under Threat

The growth of tourism has destroyed much of the lizards' former habitat. Land has been leveled to build hotels, golf courses, shops, parks, and various other tourist amenities. One islet was dynamited to improve navigation. Many of the small islets are visited by tourists who clamber about, unaware that they may be destroying lizards' nests and the vegetation.

In several Mediterranean holiday resorts, including the Balearics, deliberate eradication, including poisoning lizards around hotels, has taken place to prevent them from scaring the visitors. Although killing the lizards is illegal, it is difficult to stop. Space is at a premium in the Balearics, and setting up "biogenetic reserves," as recommended under the 1979 Berne Convention on the Conservation of European Wildlife and Natural Habitats, is difficult.

The Balearic government has researched the ecology of the lizards, but deciding which of the different forms should be protected is difficult. Saving every different island population is impossible, and some will no doubt eventually disappear. Some of the islands are also home to rare plants, birds, and seals, so establishing protected reserves would benefit more than just the lizards.

Apart from some local restrictions placed on urban and tourist developments, the situation remains largely unchanged. Further problems will inevitably arise as the lucrative tourist industry grows.

Sand Lizard

Lacerta agilis

In Britain, where all native species of lizard and snake are threatened, the sand lizard is among the most endangered. It has a restricted range and is totally dependent on a specific type of habitat. In mainland Europe the species seems to be more adaptable.

In its northern range the sand lizard is a lowland species, restricted to coastal sand dunes that offer some plant cover and sandy heathlands where heather proliferates. In Britain the lizards are confined mainly to the sand dunes of the Merseyside coast in northwestern England and the sandy heathlands of Dorset and Hampshire on the English south coast.

Shrinking Habitat

Sand lizard sites have been declining in Northern Europe since the late 19th century. In many cases the lizard's habitat has been invaded and altered by plants such as birch, pines, gorse, and bracken. However, the major threat has come from human activity. Both the Merseyside coast and the Dorset and Hampshire heathlands are popular with tourists. Although some areas are protected reserves administered by a variety of organizations, the land outside the reserves is subject to great pressure. Walkers unknowingly compact egg sites and generally disrupt the lizard's habitat. In addition, much of the range has been disturbed by new housing developments. As well as being preyed upon by foxes and hedgehogs—the sand lizard's major natural predators—the species is now also at risk from domestic cats and dogs.

Although the Dorset heaths are designated Sites of Special Scientific Interest, the need for urban development seems to have overridden all other considerations. Sand and gravel extraction for the construction industry have also destroyed a number of habitats along the south coast. Once the natural vegetation disappears, the area is invaded by grasses, bracken, gorse, and other plants that make the area unsuitable for sand lizards. Heath fires are

DATA PANEL

Sand lizard

Lacerta agilis

Family: Lacertidae

World population: Unknown

Distribution: Northern Europe, including Britain, France, Italy, south Balkans, and Iberia east to Central Asia

Habitat: Dry, sandy dunes; heaths

Size: Length head/body: up to 8 in (20 cm); tail: 8–14 in (20–30 cm)

Form: Small, robust, stout-bodied lizard. Distinct band of narrow scales runs along back. Coloration and pattern variable; Male has green along sides (vivid in spring). Dark broken stripe, bordered by 2 lighter stripes, runs along back. Female has dark blotches on gray to brown background. Underside of male is yellow-green with small, dark spots; female white to pale yellow without spots. Long, clawed digits

Diet: Insects; occasionally fruit

Breeding: One clutch of 5–14 eggs

Related endangered species: Pyrennean rock lizard *(Iberolacerta bonnali)* NT; Soutpansberg rock lizard *(Australolacerta rupicola)* NT; Schreiber's green lizard *(Lacerta schreiberi)* NT

Status: IUCN LC

a serious problem. Since the overstretched fire service has to make property protection its first priority, heath fires sometimes go unattended.

Fires, road construction, and mineral extraction not only destroy habitats, but also fragment them. As a result, lizard populations are confined to ever smaller areas where they are at greater risk of predation. Inbreeding is also more likely in small, isolated populations, leading to genetic weaknesses.

Sand lizards are a gregarious species, although fighting occurs among males in spring. They often dig holes and also make use of burrows made by small mammals. Eggs are buried in sandy, south-facing slopes and left to hatch. Adult lizards are said to eat hatchlings, which reduces numbers and can be a problem in small ranges. The young are unable to disperse to an area in which they are not in competition with their parents and therefore run more risk of being eaten.

Conservation Efforts

Several conservation agencies are working toward reversing the decline in sand lizard numbers. Ecological studies of the species exploring their requirements have been carried out. In several reserves scrub has been cleared from the lizards' habitat and other improvements made. Under the Species Recovery Plan captive-breeding programs have been set up in zoos or with private breeders, and sand lizards have been reintroduced to sites that still provide a suitable habitat. In 2012, 40 sand lizards were released at a site with suitable habitat in Surrey, England, and their progress will be closely monitored.

Sand lizards from different areas may display different coloration and also genetic variations. Populations are therefore kept separate to help ensure the breeding of healthy specimens.

However, the Species Recovery Plan will not be effective until the regulations protecting sand lizard habitat drawn up by the Berne Convention and the Wildlife and Countryside Act are applied more rigorously. Conservation agencies are trying to persuade the authorities to make greater efforts, but in some cases lack of resources is a problem. More money, for example, could pay for extra wardens to patrol and protect the reserves. Although education programs exist, convincing people that lizards and snakes are worth saving is often a difficult task.

The sand lizard is grayish brown with long, clawed digits that help it cling to rocks.

Leopard Snake

Elaphe situla

The leopard snake is often regarded as Europe's most attractive snake. Its coloration, pattern, small size, and docile nature have made it a target for private and commercial collectors, and its numbers have been further reduced by the loss of large areas of its habitat.

The genus *Elaphe* contains over 50 species, all of which are nonvenomous. Many of them are referred to as ratsnakes. Several species have been (and still are) popular vivarium subjects, frequently kept and commonly bred in captivity. Some of the familiar species are the cornsnake, Baird's ratsnake, Texas ratsnake, and yellow ratsnake. All are constrictors, preying mainly on small mammals and occasionally birds. The leopard snake, particularly when young, is said to favor lizards, although breeders have experienced no difficulty in feeding young mice to hatchlings.

The current distribution of the leopard snake is thought to be southern Italy, Croatia, Bosnia/ Herzegovina, Albania, Bulgaria, Sicily, Malta, and Greece, including some of the Greek islands, and the Crimea region of Ukraine. Its occurrence in the Caucasus is questionable—if it exists there, then it is very rare. Although apparently widespread, much of its habitat is fragmented, and it has evidently disappeared or its numbers have been reduced in many of its former locations.

Before being designated a protected species under the Berne Convention, leopard snakes regularly appeared on dealers' lists. Although once widely kept in Europe, their popularity has waned, possibly due to the availability of more exotic species and partly because of their reputation for not doing well in captivity. Captive-bred specimens are occasionally available, but their authenticity has to be proved if they are to be legally sold. Although collecting is less common today than it was, it occurs in some areas.

The leopard snake's common name comes from the row of spots or rather blotches on its body. Coloration and pattern are variable, but there are two basic forms: spotted and striped, both on a brown to light-gray background. According to breeding accounts, both spotted and striped young can hatch from a clutch, irrespective of whether parents are striped or spotted. The young are particularly brightly colored, and unlike some *Elaphe* species, the pattern and colors are retained, apart from a slight fading, into adulthood.

Leopard snakes are mainly diurnal ground-dwellers, occasionally climbing in bushes or on walls. They are

DATA PANEL

Leopard snake

Elaphe situla

Family: Colubridae

World population: Unknown

Distribution: Southeast Europe

Habitat: Mainly dry, rocky areas and stone walls; human habitations

Size: Length: 30–35 in (75–88 cm)

Form: Two basic forms: spotted and striped. Background color varies from brown to light gray. The blotches or stripes are red to brown with a dark surround. The head typically has a dark bar between the eyes; there is another bar from each eye to the upper jaw on both sides of the head. An

"arrowhead" mark of brown or red is present on top of the head. The dorsal blotches (on the back) are often in 2 rows, sometimes connected to form "saddles"

Diet: Small mammals, lizards, and birds, killed by constriction or suffocation

Breeding: One clutch of 3–5 eggs

Related endangered species: None

Status: IUCN LC

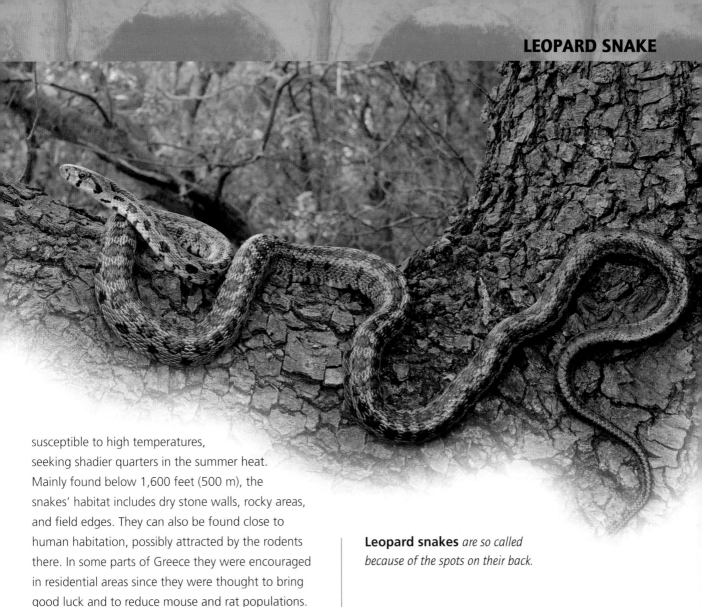

susceptible to high temperatures,
seeking shadier quarters in the summer heat.
Mainly found below 1,600 feet (500 m), the
snakes' habitat includes dry stone walls, rocky areas,
and field edges. They can also be found close to
human habitation, possibly attracted by the rodents
there. In some parts of Greece they were encouraged
in residential areas since they were thought to bring
good luck and to reduce mouse and rat populations.

When disturbed, the leopard snake rapidly vibrates
its tail tip. This is a bluff meant to scare attackers and
not a sign that it is venomous. The same display in
rattlesnakes often precedes a poisonous strike.

Harmful Developments

Many of the countries inhabited by leopard snakes
have traditionally had a high level of poverty, resulting
in the rapid growth of industry to boost employment.
Intensification of agriculture has also threatened
the snake's survival with clearing of lowland forest
and scrubland to make way for livestock and crops.
Several of the countries have a pleasant Mediterranean
climate, which attracts thousands of tourists every year.
The construction of tourist facilities—including roads—

Leopard snakes *are so called*
because of the spots on their back.

has had a devastating impact on natural habitats. In
addition, many people have an ingrained fear of snakes
and cannot be convinced that they are harmless. In
tourist areas leopard snakes, like other snakes and
lizards, are often eradicated.

The leopard snake is listed by the IUCN as of
Least Concern. However, populations are declining
as its habitat is reduced in much of its former range.
Further field studies on its distribution, population
size, and ecology are needed, but financial and
political considerations are likely to prevent or delay
them. For a declining species its low reproductive rate
is a disadvantage to recovery. Any captive-breeding
programs are in the hands of private individuals, and as
yet there is no organized recovery program.

Great Crested Newt

Triturus cristatus

Although the great crested newt is widely distributed across Europe, the species has declined over much of its range. Changes in land use and agricultural practices over the last 50 years have destroyed much of its pond and woodland habitat.

The great crested newt of northwestern Europe—along with other European newts of the genus *Triturus*—gets its name from the large, deeply notched crest that runs along the back of the breeding male. The *Triturus* newts are unique among tailed amphibians: During the breeding season the males develop elaborate decorations that serve to attract and stimulate females during courtship.

Although great crested newts spend much of their lives on land, breeding takes place in water. Adults migrate to ponds in early spring. Females start the breeding season already full of large, yolk-filled eggs. It takes the males several weeks to fully develop their deep tail and crest, features that play an important part in the mating process. Males that emerge from their winter hibernation with larger fat reserves develop larger crests, and it is likely that they are more attractive to females.

Mating usually occurs at dusk. The male takes up a position in front of the female and displays to her with rhythmic beats of his tail. If the female responds by moving toward him, the male deposits a package of sperm, called a spermatophore, on the floor of the pond. The female then moves over it and picks it up with her open cloaca (cavity into which the genital ducts open).

Two or three days after mating the female begins to lay her eggs, a process that takes many weeks. Great crested newts usually produce between 150 and 200 eggs, each of which is laid individually and carefully wrapped in the leaf of a water plant. After two to three weeks the eggs hatch into tiny larvae, which, once they have used up their reserves of yolk, start to feed on tiny aquatic animals, such as water fleas. Larval development takes two to three months, and the young emerge from their pond as miniature adults in late summer and fall. Females mate several times during the breeding season, interrupting egg-laying to replenish their supplies of sperm.

Risk Factors

Together with its close relative, the marbled newt, the great crested newt has a remarkable abnormality of its chromosomes. As a result, 50 percent of its young die as early embryos. This is one reason, perhaps, why great crested newts have declined more rapidly than other European newt species.

Predation is not a significant problem for adult great crested newts. When handled, glands in their skin produce a bitter, milky secretion that humans and potential predators, such as water birds and hedgehogs, find highly distasteful. In addition, the bright orange and black pattern on the belly appears to warn off predators.

However, great crested newts are at risk from habitat alteration and destruction. The main problem has been changes in land use since World War II. Woodlands have been cleared, hedges destroyed, and land drained to make way for crops and livestock. Ponds, which were a common

feature of the European landscape, have been filled in. In some parts of Britain, for example, 90 percent of farm ponds have disappeared in the last 50 years.

Another threat to great crested and other newt species comes from fish that eat newt larvae. The eggs and larvae of crested newts are also sensitive to a variety of pollutants, such as herbicides and pesticides.

In the southern parts of its range the great crested newt is found in a number of forms that differ from the northern form in having longer bodies, shorter legs, and a different shape of crest on the male. Such forms are now recognized as three distinct species: the Italian crested newt, the Danube crested newt, and the southern crested newt. All are threatened by habitat loss and protected, to varying degrees, by national and European laws.

At the southwestern edge of its distribution, however, the great crested newt is expanding its range. In some parts of France it appears to be adapting to new patterns of land use and is even spreading into ponds previously used only by marbled newts.

DATA PANEL

Great crested newt

Triturus cristatus

Family: Salamandridae

World population: Unknown

Distribution: Northwestern Europe

Habitat: Woodland, scrub, and hedgerows close to ponds, lakes, or ditches

Size: Length: male 3.9–5.5 in (10–14 cm); female 3.9–6.3 in (10–16 cm)

Form: Dark gray or brown newt with large black spots on upperside; bright orange underside with black spots. In breeding season male (only) has large, dorsal crest and deep tail with white stripe

Diet: Small invertebrates

Breeding: Mates in spring and early summer. Between 70 and 600 (usually 150–200) eggs laid; larvae hatch after 2-week gestation; young develop over 2–3 months. Life span up to 16 years

Related endangered species: Danube crested newt (*Triturus dobrogicus*) NT

Status: IUCN LC

In the breeding *season the male great crested newt develops a distinctive crest, which he displays during courtship. The tail has a conspicuous pale stripe that shows up clearly in the dim light of dusk —when mating occurs.*

Natterjack Toad

Bufo calamita

A species with habitat requirements that are different from other frogs and toads, the natterjack toad has disappeared from much of its range as a result of degradation and loss of its habitat.

The natterjack toad runs rather than hops across the ground; unlike most toads, it has small hindlimbs that are too weak for hopping or jumping. It has a horny tubercle on each of its hind feet, and it uses them to dig, at remarkable speed, into the soft, sandy soils it inhabits. It lives in its burrow by day, digging deep enough to reach damp soil. As a result, natterjacks are able to thrive in habitats that are very dry at the surface. They also use their burrows when hibernating during the winter. Individual natterjacks show attachment to their burrows, returning to the same site each day.

As with most toads, the natterjack has dry, warty skin, and in some individuals the warts are marked by red spots. Its most characteristic feature is the thin, pale-yellow stripe that runs down the middle of its back, the function of which is not known. The skin on its belly is granular (grainy) and able to take up water from damp spots in the ground. In contrast to common toads, in which the females are considerably larger than the males, male and female natterjacks are similar in size. One difference between the sexes is the swollen pad that male natterjacks develop on their thumbs during the breeding season; the pads enable the male to clasp the female firmly during mating and thereby to resist the attempts of rival males to displace him.

Prolonged Breeding Season

Natterjacks emerge to breed later in the spring than other European frogs and toads—as late as April in Britain. Breeding activity may continue, somewhat sporadically, until August in years when breeding ponds do not dry out in the summer. Tadpoles may metamorphose into adults at any time between June and September. Some individuals of both sexes may breed more than once during extended breeding seasons. In some years, however, ponds evaporate before the tadpoles have completed their development, in which case no young natterjacks are produced. Adults can live for up to

---

DATA PANEL

Natterjack toad

Bufo calamita

Family: Bufonidae

World population: Unknown

Distribution: Western and northern Europe

Habitat: Open landscapes with light, sandy soil, including heathland and sand dunes

Size: Length: 2–4 in (5–10 cm)

Form: Gray or green above with narrow yellow stripe down middle of back; pale on belly. Warty skin; prominent parotid glands on head. Eye has green iris with horizontal pupil. Hard tubercles on hind feet

Diet: Beetles and other small invertebrates

Breeding: Spring and summer; males call to attract females; eggs laid in long strings

Related endangered species: Amargosa toad (*Bufo nelsoni*) EN; Amatola toad (*B. amatolicus*) VU; black toad (*B. exsul*) VU; Houston toad (*B. houstonensis*) EN; western toad (*B. boreas*) EN; Yosemite toad (*B. canorus*) EN

Status: IUCN LC

17 years, so that individuals are likely to experience some good and some bad breeding seasons during their lives.

Males have a loud, churring call that humans can hear from as far away as 0.6 miles (1 km). While calling, the male inflates a large vocal sac under his chin. Females approach, and amplexus (the mating embrace) is followed by egg laying, in which two long strings of eggs are deposited among water plants. Natterjack egg strings differ from those of common toads in having a single rather than a double row of eggs. One female lays between 2,800 and 4,000 eggs at a time. Natterjack eggs, tadpoles, and adults are distasteful to potential predators and so are protected.

Competition Among Males

Males vary in their ability to sustain the energetic level of calling that is necessary to attract females. In larger breeding populations some males do not call at all but instead show "satellite" behavior, sitting silently by the side of a calling male and trying to intercept females that approach. In very large populations, such as those found in some parts of Spain, calling males can attract so many satellites that no females are able to reach

them. In this situation all males abandon calling as a means of obtaining females, and mating becomes a competitive scramble like that seen in common toads.

Specific Habitat Requirements

Natterjacks prefer open habitats such as heathland and coastal sand dunes that are too dry for common frogs and toads. They suffer if they happen to breed in the same ponds as other frogs and toads because their tadpoles, hatching out several weeks later, cannot compete with the larger tadpoles of their rivals.

Natterjacks have disappeared from many parts of their range, mainly because their habitat has been degraded or destroyed. Where heathland has been replaced by woodland, common frogs and toads have moved in. In some areas natterjacks have been badly affected by pollution from pesticides and fertilizers used on farmland. The species is particularly endangered at the extremes of its range, in Britain, Scandinavia, Germany, and Poland.

The natterjack toad *has dry, warty skin, sometimes marked with red spots. It can take up moisture from the ground through the granular skin on its belly.*

Valencia Toothcarp

Valencia hispanica

The Valencia toothcarp is rated as one of the 24 most endangered species of vertebrate in the world. Ten freshwater locations close to the Mediterranean coast of the Valencia region in Spain hold the last populations of this fish.

The Valencia toothcarp is a small, minnowlike fish. It is one of only a few European species of egg-laying killifish, most of the other species occurring in Africa and the New World. Some species of toothcarp are low in number, and many are threatened in the wild.

Toothcarp Characteristics

Despite the inclusion of "carp" in their name, toothcarps are not related to the carps proper that—with the minnows and their relatives—constitute the family Cyprinidae of the order Cypriniformes. The illusion of relatedness is reinforced by the name of one toothcarp family, the Cyprinodontidae. The Cyprinodontidae, along with their relatives in other toothcarp families (like the Valenciidae to which the Valencia toothcarp belongs), are all members of the order Cyprinodontiformes.

Numerous anatomical and other characteristics separate the order Cypriniformes from the order Cyprinodontiformes. For example, carps and their relatives within the Cypriniformes do not have any jaw teeth, while the toothcarps most certainly do, hence their name. Reproductively, too, there are significant differences. Cypriniformes characteristically produce relatively large numbers of eggs (several hundred thousand per spawning in the case of the larger species). The Cyprinodontiformes, on the other hand, produce few, with numbers sometimes being as low as five or six.

Within the toothcarps there are two subdivisions. One is the livebearing toothcarps, which—as their name suggests—do not lay eggs but give birth to fully formed young. The other is the egg-laying toothcarps, which lay eggs. A few egg-laying carp species employ internal fertilization, just as the livebearing toothcarps do. The Valencia toothcarp belongs to the egg-laying toothcarps.

DATA PANEL

Valencia toothcarp (samaruc)

Valencia hispanica

Family: Valenciidae

World population: Unknown, but restricted to just 10 populations

Distribution: Spain: Peñiscola (in Castellón); Albufera de Valencia (just south of Valencia); Pego-Oliva (between Valencia and Alicante)

Habitat: Clean, clear, slow-flowing or standing waters with dense aquatic vegetation

Size: Female up to 2.8 in (7 cm); male smaller

Form: Elongated, laterally compressed body; large eyes; well-formed, rounded fins. Peñiscola males are uniform bluish-green; those from other localities have brown sheen in anterior half of body. All carry thin, vertical stripes, particularly in posterior half of body. Females drabber (browner) overall

Diet: Small aquatic invertebrates; small aerial insects that may fall into the water

Breeding: Two peaks of activity in spawning season: early spring and end of summer. Males establish territories that are visited by females. Eggs laid among fine-leaved vegetation; hatching takes about 1 week

Related endangered species: Corfu toothcarp (*Valencia letourneuxi*) CR

Status: IUCN CR

The Valencia toothcarp
*prefers clean, slow-flowing water
with plenty of vegetation. Its
diet includes small insects such
as mosquitoes.*

Survival Pressures

In its natural habitat the Valencia
toothcarp tends to occupy clean, clear,
slow-flowing or static, well-vegetated
bodies of water. It is also known to
tolerate high levels of salt, an indication
that in former days it occupied brackish
(salty) regions along the coast. However, all
the current known localities for the species are
strictly freshwater ones.

Because of its requirements for clean, clear
water the Valencia toothcarp has been unable to
adapt to the consequences of an expanding human
population in the region. The tourist industry is a
major threat to the fish's habitat. The construction of
tourist developments, for example, has often led to the
destruction of toothcarp habitat and increased levels of
water pollution. The channeling of water for irrigation
or other water-supply projects is another threat to the
fish's survival.

The Valencia toothcarp is not only at risk from
human threats. Even where water and other habitat
conditions favor the survival of the species, introduced
species have put the fish under severe pressure. For
example, the mosquitofish—itself a toothcarp (but
a livebearing one)—was introduced into Spain in
the early 1920s as a biological means of controlling
malarial mosquitoes. The mosquitofish competes with
the Valencia toothcarp for space and food. In addition,
a female mosquitofish can store sperm from a single
mating and use it to fertilize a series of egg batches
during the breeding season. As a result, she produces
far larger numbers of young than the Valencia female.
Introduced predators also pose a threat.

Recovery Plans

Saving a species that faces such diverse and intense
pressures presents a complex challenge. At one time the
fish was known from just three locations. One obvious
measure was captive breeding, and captive-bred stocks
now exist in Spain and elsewhere. The release of
captive-bred Valencia toothcarp into suitable habitats in
the region has helped increase their numbers. However,
more permanent habitat-based measures are needed if
the species is to survive in the wild.

Of prime importance is the protection of the
fish's existing locations and other suitable habitat in
the region that an expanding population of Valencia
toothcarp can recolonize in the future. Also important
has been the establishment of reserves in areas that
used to be inhabited by these fish.

Large Blue Butterfly

Maculinea arion

The large butterfly is so called because of the distinctive turquoise-blue sheen on parts of its wings. Its life cycle is inextricably linked with other insect species and plant life, making it vulnerable to natural or human disturbance of any kind.

The large blue butterfly is found scattered over Europe, particularly in coastal areas. It is capable of vigorous flight, despite its fragile appearance, and can navigate strong winds that would make flying difficult for other insects.

Like other butterflies, the large blue begins life as an egg. The female lays her clutch on the leaves of wild thyme, having carefully selected the site. As well as having the right microclimate, or balance of humidity, protection, and temperature, the bush must be close to or on top of an ant's nest, because of the large blue's dependency on ant larvae for food.

The eggs hatch into caterpillars—the second stage of the butterfly's life cycle. When they first emerge, the caterpillars are well camouflaged, closely resembling the white thyme blossom on which they feed. They molt, or shed their skin, up to four times, growing rapidly after the earlier molts. After the second they become carnivorous, leaving the thyme plant to hunt for insects. They may also feed on caterpillars of the same species.

At the caterpillar stage the large blue butterfly frequently encounters ants. A relationship with the ant community develops, and the caterpillar begins to rely for its development on ant larvae. The ants, in turn, benefit from the caterpillar's dependency, relishing the honeydew secreted by a gland on its abdomen. The ant strokes the gland to stimulate secretion and drinks the honeydew produced. The caterpillar then hunches up, signaling that it is ready to be carried to the ants' nest. The ants take the caterpillar deep down into the nest, where it is tended to by worker ants and milked for honeydew. Secure in the nest, the caterpillar starts to feed on ant larvae. Incredibly, the worker ants who usually guard the larvae fiercely allow the predation to carry on. Cases of ant colonies dying out because they could not support a large volume of large blue caterpillars have been recorded.

After about six weeks the caterpillar has changed into a white, fleshy, grublike animal. In this state it hibernates throughout the winter, developing into a chrysalis (pupa) in May. After three weeks' pupation, during which it undergoes dramatic

DATA PANEL

Large blue butterfly

Maculinea arion

Family: Lycaenidae

World population: Unknown

Distribution: Europe

Habitat: Coastal areas and downland; also mountains up to 6,560 ft (2,000m)

Size: Length: 0.7 in (1.7 cm); wingspan: 1.6 in (4 cm)

Form: Body covered in fine scales. Two pairs of conspicuous wings with black patterns on blue background; underside of wings brown with black marks (females have more marks on front wings than males); each mark is surrounded by a fine white ring

Diet: At the caterpillar stage the large blue butterfly eats wild thyme blossom, insects (including other caterpillars), and ant larvae. Adults feed on flower nectar and other liquids

Breeding: Female lays eggs in wild thyme flowers. Egg develops into caterpillar (larva), then chrysalis (pupa), and finally adult butterfly. Adults emerge as separate sexes

Related endangered species: Large copper butterfly (*Lycaena dispar*) NT; Avalon hairstreak butterfly (*Strymon avalona*) VU

Status: IUCN NT

internal changes,
it emerges from its
cocoon as an adult
large blue and leaves
the ants' nest, making
its way through the maze
of passages until it reaches
the outside world. The larvae
of most other blue butterfly species
have the honey glands and attract ants, but unlike
the large blue, are not taken into the ants' nests.

Dangers

The large blue butterfly's dependence on particular
plant and insect life makes survival problematic. Its
preference for just one type of plant for egg laying
means that it is totally reliant on an abundance of
wild thyme. Scarcity of the plant because of human
encroachment could severely threaten the species.
Wild thyme also appears to offer the right microclimate
for speedy development of the eggs, thereby reducing
exposure to predators. Another concern is the

The large blue butterfly *may settle on*
vegetation to bask in the sun after it has fed
on the nectar from flowers.

tendency of the caterpillars to feed on their own kind
when they become carnivorous. Such behavior can have
an adverse effect on numbers reaching adulthood.

Codependency with ants is essential to the life cycle
of the large blue. In parts of Europe human disturbance
of heathland, by building, for example, has wiped
out ant nests. Such activity has limited the number of
suitable sites for the large blue butterfly.

Large Copper Butterfly

Lycaena dispar

The large copper butterfly was introduced into Britain from the Netherlands in 1927 to replace the native established English race that had become extinct in about 1850. The race native to the Netherlands is the largest; it is found in marshy areas in the north of that country.

The large copper butterfly is an example of a species that is highly adapted to a particular habitat. It relies on the availability of fens and marshes, favoring only one species of marsh vegetation: the great water dock plant. The butterfly uses the plant as a site for egg laying and as a source of food. The caterpillars may also feed on sorrel.

Once the eggs have been laid, the developing larvae (caterpillars) feed on the underside of the leaves, remaining hidden from view. As they feed they gradually cut holes in the leaves. As winter approaches, they hibernate, changing from the soft green color of the feeding phase to the brownish-purple of the hibernating phase. The lack of fresh chlorophyll (green pigment) in the leaves is probably the cause of this. To some extent their drab color matches that of the decaying leaves of the great water dock as the plant dies down in winter.

Astonishingly, the larvae can withstand immersion in water during the winter floods. With the onset of spring the larvae resume feeding and also regain their soft green color. Immediately before they pupate, the caterpillars spin a pad of silk thread on a leaf and attach themselves to it.

Large copper butterfly larvae do not secrete honeydew and lack the honey gland found in some species. Instead, they produce a sweet secretion from the skin. This attracts ants that protect the larvae from various parasites and predators.

Shrinking Habitat

The large copper butterfly was once fairly widespread in the fens of East Anglia, Lincolnshire, and Cambridgeshire in eastern England. However, habitat destruction

DATA PANEL

Large copper butterfly

Lycaena dispar

Family: Lycaenidae

World population: Unknown

Distribution: Europe

Habitat: Fen (low-lying, flat marshy land) and marsh

Size: Length head/body: 0.8 in (1.7 cm); wingspan: 1.8 in (4.3 cm)

Form: Two pairs of conspicuous wings. Males and females have (different) copper and black-colored markings on the upper wings; underside of wings similar in both sexes. Wings and body are covered with fine scales

Diet: Adults feed on liquids such as nectar, using sucking mouthparts. Larvae (caterpillars) feed on leaves of the great water dock

Breeding: Eggs laid in summer develop into larvae, which live through the winter. Pupae develop and metamorphose into males or females in late June

Related endangered species: Hermes copper (*Lycaena hermes*) VU

Status: IUCN NT

and overcollection by zealous butterfly enthusiasts (supported by local people selling them) exerted pressure on the large copper and contributed to its extinction. The continental race of large copper butterfly, which was introduced to Britain from the Netherlands, became established for a while in the 1970s but could not sustain itself and died out again; if attempts had been made to conserve the habitat of the English race when it was dying out in the late 1840s, it might still be alive.

The large copper butterfly's reliance on a particular habitat makes the species extremely vulnerable to environmental change. Drainage of wetlands

and woodland development destroy the vegetation required by the larvae. In addition, suitable sites are often widely separated from each other by inhospitable habitat, so expansion of populations is difficult.

Conservation Plan

As long as the full life cycle of the large copper butterfly is understood and the needs of the egg-laying adults and larvae are catered to, conservation of the species is perfectly possible. Although the importance of habitat preservation was not appreciated in the mid-19th century, the butterfly is now the subject of a scientific study to work out whether it can be reestablished in the UK, where hopefully it will flourish in the future.

The large copper butterfly
has brilliantly colored black and copper markings and is capable of strong, rapid flight.

Categories of Threat

The status categories that appear in the data panel for each species throughout this book are based on those published by the International Union for the Conservation of Nature (IUCN). They provide a useful guide to the current status of the species in the wild, and governments throughout the world use them when assessing conservation priorities and in policy making. However, they do not provide automatic legal protection for the species.

Animals are placed in the appropriate category after scientific research. More species are being added all the time, and animals can be moved from one category to another as their circumstances change.

Extinct (EX)

A group of animals is classified as EX when there is no reasonable doubt that the last individual has died.

Extinct in the Wild (EW)

Animals in this category are known to survive only in captivity or as a population established artificially by introduction somewhere well outside its former range. A species is categorized as EW when exhaustive surveys throughout the areas where it used to occur consistently fail to record a single individual. It is important that such searches be carried out over all of the available habitat and during a season or time of day when the animals should be present.

Critically Endangered (CR)

The category CR includes animals facing an extremely high risk of extinction in the wild in the immediate future. It includes any of the following:

- Any species with fewer than 50 individuals, even if the population is stable.
- Any species with fewer than 250 individuals if the population is declining, badly fragmented, or all in one vulnerable group.
- Animals from larger populations that have declined by 80 percent within 10 years (or are predicted to do so) or three generations, whichever is the longer.

The IUCN categories

of threat. The system displayed has operated for new and reviewed assessments since January 2001.

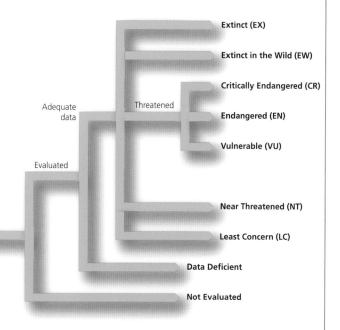

Extinct (EX)
Extinct in the Wild (EW)
Critically Endangered (CR)
Endangered (EN)
Vulnerable (VU)
Near Threatened (NT)
Least Concern (LC)
Data Deficient
Not Evaluated

Adequate data
Threatened
Evaluated

• Species living in a very small area—defined as under 39 square miles (100 sq. km).

Endangered (EN)

A species is EN when it is not CR but is nevertheless facing a very high risk of extinction in the wild in the near future. It includes any of the following:

• A species with fewer than 250 individuals remaining, even if the population is stable.

• Any species with fewer than 2,500 individuals if the population is declining, badly fragmented, or all in one vulnerable subpopulation.

• A species whose population is known or expected to decline by 50 percent within 10 years or three generations, whichever is the longer.

• A species whose range is under 1,900 square miles (5,000 sq. km), and whose range, numbers, or population levels are declining, fragmented, or fluctuating wildly.

• Species for which there is a more than 20 percent likelihood of extinction in the next 20 years or five generations, whichever is the longer.

Vulnerable (VU)

A species is VU when it is not CR or EN but is facing a high risk of extinction in the wild in the medium-term future. It includes any of the following:

• A species with fewer than 1,000 mature individuals remaining, even if the population is stable.

• Any species with fewer than 10,000 individuals if the population is declining, badly fragmented, or all in one vulnerable subpopulation.

The Eurasian otter *(left) is one animal whose status has been changed in recent years—from Vulnerable to Near Threatened. This change was made because the rate of decline of its population has slowed as conservation measures take effect.*

• A species whose population is known, believed, or expected to decline by 20 percent within 10 years or three generations, whichever is the longer.

• A species whose range is less than 772 square miles (2,000 sq. km), and whose range, numbers, or population structure are declining, fragmented, or fluctuating wildly.

• Species for which there is a more than 10 percent likelihood of extinction in the next 100 years.

Near Threatened/Least Concern (since 2001)

In January 2001 the classification of lower-risk species was changed. Near Threatened (NT) and Least Concern (LC) were introduced as separate categories. They replaced the previous Lower Risk (LR) category with its subdivisions of Conservation Dependent (LRcd), Near Threatened (LRnt), and Least Concern (LRlc). From January 2001 all new assessments and reassessments must adopt NT or LC if relevant. But the older categories still apply to some animals until they are reassessed, and will also be found in this book.

• Near Threatened (NT)
Animals that do not qualify for CR, EN, or VU categories now but are close to qualifying or are likely to qualify for a threatened category in the future.

• Least Concern (LC)
Animals that have been evaluated and do not qualify for CR, EN, VU, or NT categories.

Lower Risk (before 2001)

• Conservation Dependent (LRcd)
Animals whose survival depends on an existing conservation program.

• Near Threatened (LRnt)
Animals for which there is no conservation program but that are close to qualifying for VU category.

• Least Concern (LRlc)
Species that are not conservation dependent or near threatened.

The destruction *of reed beds led to a decline in Eurasian bittern numbers in many countries. Nevertheless, scientists still consider the species to be of Least Concern because it breeds across an enormous area of Europe and Asia.*

Data Deficient (DD)

A species or population is DD when there is not enough information on abundance and distribution to assess the risk of extinction. In some cases, when the species is thought to live only in a small area, or a considerable period of time has passed since the species was last recorded, it may be placed in a threatened category as a precaution.

Not Evaluated (NE)

Such animals have not yet been assessed.

Note: a colored panel in each entry in this book indicates the current level of threat to the species. The two new categories (NT and LC) include the earlier Lower Risk categories (LRcd and LRnt); the old LRlc is included along with Data Deficient (DD) and Not Evaluated (NE) under "Other," abbreviated to "O."

CITES *lists animals in the major groups in three Appendices, depending on the level of threat posed by international trade.*

	Appendix I	Appendix II	Appendix III
Mammals	297 species 23 subspecies 2 populations	492 species 5 subspecies 5 populations	44 species 10 subspecies
Birds	156 species 11 subspecies 2 populations	1,275 species 2 subspecies	24 species
Reptiles	76 species 5 subspecies 1 population	582 species 6 populations	56 species
Amphibians	17 species	113 species	1 species
Fish	15 species	81 species	
Invertebrates	64 species 5 subspecies	2,142 species 1 subspecies	17 species 3 subspecies

CITES APPENDICES

Appendix I lists the most endangered of traded species, namely those that are threatened with extinction and will be harmed by continued trade. These species are usually protected in their native countries and can only be imported or exported with a special permit. Permits are required to cover the whole transaction—both exporter and importer must prove that there is a compelling scientific justification for moving the animal from one country to another. This includes transferring animals between zoos for breeding purposes. Permits are only issued when it can be proved that the animal was legally acquired and that the remaining population will not be harmed by the loss.

Appendix II includes species not currently threatened with extinction but could easily become so if trade is not carefully controlled. Some common animals are listed here if they resemble endangered species so closely that criminals could try to sell the rare species pretending they were a similar common one. Permits are required to export such animals, with requirements similar to those Appendix I species.

Appendix III species are those that are at risk or protected in at least one country. Other nations may be allowed to trade in animals or products, but they may need to prove that they come from safe populations.

CITES designations are not always the same for every country. In some cases individual countries can apply for special permission to trade in a listed species. For example, they might have a safe population of an animal that is very rare elsewhere. Some African countries periodically apply for permission to export large quantities of elephant tusks that have been in storage for years, or that are the product of a legal cull of elephants. This is controversial because it creates an opportunity for criminals to dispose of black market ivory by passing it off as coming from one of those countries where elephant products are allowed to be exported. The African elephant, for example, is listed as CITES I, II, and III, depending on the country location of the different populations.

Organizations

The human race is undoubtedly nature's worst enemy, but we can also help limit the damage caused by the rapid increase in our numbers and activities. There have always been people eager to protect the world's beautiful places and to preserve its most special animals, but it is only quite recently that the conservation message has begun to have a real effect on everyday life, government policy, industry, and agriculture.

Early conservationists were concerned with preserving nature for the benefit of people. They acted with an instinctive sense of what was good for nature and people, arguing for the preservation of wilderness and animals in the same way as others argued for the conservation of historic buildings or gardens. The study of ecology and environmental science did not really take off until the mid-20th century, and it took a long time for the true scale of our effect on the natural world to become apparent. Today the conservation of wildlife is based on far greater scientific understanding, but the situation has become much more complex and urgent in the face of human development.

By the mid-20th century extinction was becoming an immediate threat. Animals such as the passenger pigeon, quagga, and thylacine had disappeared despite last-minute attempts to save them. More and more species were discovered to be at risk, and species-focused conservation groups began to appear. In the early days there was little that any of these organizations could do but campaign against direct killing. Later they became a kind of conservation emergency service—rushing to the aid of seriously threatened animals in an attempt to save the species. But as time went on, broader environmental issues began to receive the urgent attention they needed. Research showed time and time again that saving species almost always comes down to addressing the problem of habitat loss. The world is short of space, and ensuring that there is enough for all the species is very difficult.

Conservation is not just about animals and plants, nor even the protection of whole ecological systems. Conservation issues are so broad that they touch almost every aspect of our lives, and successful measures often depend on the expertise of biologists, ecologists, economists, diplomats, lawyers, social scientists, and businesspeople. Conservation is all about cooperation and teamwork. Often it is also about helping people benefit from taking care of their wildlife. The organizations involved vary from small groups of a few dozen enthusiasts in local communities to vast, multinational operations.

With so much activity based in different countries, it is important to have a worldwide overview—some way of coordinating what goes on in different parts of the planet. That is the role of the International Union for the Conservation of Nature (IUCN), also referred to as the World Conservation Union. It began life as the International Union for the Preservation of Nature in 1948, becoming the IUCN in 1956. It is relatively new compared to the Sierra Club, Flora and Fauna International, and the Royal Society for the Protection of Birds. It was remarkable in that its founder members included governments, government agencies, and nongovernmental organizations. In the years following the appalling destruction of World War II, the IUCN was born out of a desire to draw a line under the horrors of the past and to act together to safeguard the future.

The mission of the IUCN is to influence, encourage, and assist societies throughout the world to conserve the diversity of nature and natural systems. It seeks to ensure that the use of natural resources is fair and ecologically sustainable. Based in Switzerland, the IUCN

The United Nations *has made Coto Doñana National Park, Spain, a World Heritage site because of its populations of endangered animals, including Iberian lynx, Spanish imperial eagle, and white-headed duck.*

has over 1,000 permanent staff and the help of 11,000 volunteer experts from about 180 countries. The work of the IUCN is split into six commissions, which deal with protected areas, policy-making, ecosystem management, education, environmental law, and species survival. The Species Survival Commission (SSC) has almost 7,000 members, all experts in the study of plants and animals. Within the SSC there are Specialist Groups concerned with the conservation of different types of animals, from cats to flamingos, deer, ducks, bats, and crocodiles. Some particularly well-studied animals, such as the African elephant and the polar bear, have their own specialist groups.

Perhaps the best-known role of the IUCN SSC is in the production of the Red Data Books, or Red Lists. First published in 1966, the books were designed to

be easily updated, with details of each species on a different page that could be removed and replaced as new information came to light.

By 2013 the Red Lists include information on about 53,000 types of animal, of which more than 11,000 are threatened with extinction. Gathering this amount of information together is a huge task, but it provides an invaluable conservation resource. The Red Lists are continually updated and are now available online. The Red Lists are the basis for the categories of threat used in this book.

CITES is the Convention on International Trade in Endangered Species of Wild Fauna and Flora (also known as the Washington Convention, since it first came into force after an international meeting in Washington D.C. in 1973). Currently 175 nations have agreed to implement the CITES regulations. Exceptions to the convention include Iraq and North Korea, which, for the time being at least, have few trading links with the rest of the world. Trading in animals and their body parts has been a major factor in the decline of some of the world's rarest species. The IUCN categories draw attention to the status of rare species, but they do not confer any legal protection. That is done through national laws.

Conventions serve as international laws. In the case of CITES, lists (called Appendices) are agreed on internationally and reviewed every few years. The Appendices list the species that are threatened by international trade. Animals are assigned to Appendix I when all trade is forbidden. Any specimens of these species, alive or dead (or skins, feathers, etc.), will be confiscated by customs at international borders, seaports, or airports. Appendix II species can be traded internationally, but only under strict controls. Wildlife trade is often valuable in the rural economy, and this raises difficult questions about the relative importance of animals and people. Nevertheless, traders who ignore CITES rules risk heavy fines or imprisonment. Some rare species—even those with the highest IUCN categories (many bats and frogs, for example)—may have no CITES protection simply because they have no commercial value. Trade is then not really a threat.

WILDLIFE CONSERVATION ORGANIZATIONS

BirdLife International
BirdLife International is a partnership of 60 organizations working in more than 100 countries. Most partners are national nongovernmental conservation groups. Others include large bird charities. By working within BirdLife International, even small organizations can be effective globally as well as on a local scale.
www.birdlife.org

Conservation International (CI)
Founded in 1987, Conservation International works closely with the IUCN and has a similar multinational approach.
www.conservation.org

Durrell Wildlife Conservation Trust (DWCT)
The Durrell Wildlife Conservation Trust was founded by the British naturalist and author Gerald Durrell in 1963. The trust is based at Durrell's zoo on Jersey in the Channel Islands. Jersey Zoo and the DWCT were instrumental in saving many species from extinction, including the pink pigeon, Mauritius kestrel, Waldrapp ibis, St. Lucia parrot, and Telfair's skink.
www.durrell.org

Fauna & Flora International (FFI)
Founded in 1903, this organization has had various name changes. It began life as a society for protecting large mammals, but has broadened its scope. It was involved in saving the Arabian oryx from extinction.
www.fauna-flora.org

National Audubon Society
John James Audubon was an American naturalist and wildlife artist who died in 1851, 35 years before the society that bears his name was founded. The first Audubon Society was established by George Bird Grinnell in protest against the appalling overkill of birds for meat, feathers, and sport. By the end of the 19th century there were Audubon Societies in 15 states, and they later became part of the National Audubon Society, which funds scientific research programs, publishes magazines and journals, manages wildlife sanctuaries, and advises state and federal governments on conservation.
www.audubon.org

The Sierra Club
The Sierra Club was started in 1892 by John Muir. It was through Muir's efforts that the first national parks, including Yosemite, Sequoia, and Mount Rainier, were established. Today the Sierra Club remains dedicated to the preservation of wild places for the benefit of wildlife and people.
www.sierraclub.org

World Wide Fund for Nature (WWF)
The World Wide Fund for Nature, formerly the World Wildlife Fund, was born in 1961. It was a joint venture between the IUCN, several existing conservation organizations, and a number of successful businesspeople. WWF was big, well funded, and high profile from the beginning. Its familiar giant panda emblem is instantly recognizable.
www.wwf.org

More Endangered Animals

This is the second series of Facts at Your Fingertips: Endangered Animals. Many other endangered animals were included in the first series, which was broken down by animal class, as follows:

BIRDS

Northern Brown
   Kiwi
Galápagos Penguin
Bermuda Petrel
Andean Flamingo
Northern Bald Ibis
White-headed Duck
Nene
Philippine Eagle
Spanish Imperial
   Eagle
Red Kite
California Condor
Mauritius Kestrel
Whooping Crane
Takahe
Kakapo
Hyacinth Macaw
Pink Pigeon
Spotted Owl
Bee Hummingbird
Regent Honeyeater
Blue Bird of Paradise
Raso Lark
Gouldian Finch

FISH

Coelacanth
Great White Shark
Common Sturgeon
Danube Salmon
Lake Victoria
   Haplochromine
   Cichlids
Dragon Fish
Silver Shark
Whale Shark
Northern Bluefin
   Tuna

Masked Angelfish
Big Scale Archerfish
Bandula Barb
Mekong Giant
   Catfish
Alabama Cavefish
Blind Cave Characin
Atlantic Cod
Mountain Blackside
   Dace
Lesser Spiny Eel
Australian Lungfish
Paddlefish
Ornate Paradisefish
Knysna Seahorse
Spring Pygmy
   Sunfish

INVERTEBRATES

Broad Sea Fan
Giant Gippsland
   Earthworm
Edible Sea-Urchin
Velvet Worms
Southern Damselfly
Orange-spotted
   Emerald
Red-kneed
   Tarantula
Kauai Cave Wolf
   Spider
Great Raft Spider
European Red
   Wood Ant
Hermit Beetle
Blue Ground Beetle
Birdwing Butterfly
Apollo Butterfly
Avalon Hairstreak
   Butterfly

Hermes Copper
   Butterfly
Giant Clam
California Bay
   Pea Crab
Horseshoe Crab
Cushion Star
Freshwater Mussel
Starlet Sea
   Anemone
Partula Snails

MAMMALS OF THE NORTHERN HEMISPHERE

Asiatic Lion
Tiger
Clouded Leopard
Iberian Lynx
Florida Panther
Wildcat
Gray Wolf
Swift Fox
Polar Bear
Giant Panda
European Mink
Pine Marten
Black-footed Ferret
Wolverine
Sea Otter
Steller's Sea Lion
Mediterranean
   Monk Seal
Florida Manatee
Przewalski's
   Wild Horse
American Bison
Arabian Oryx
Wild Yak
Ryukyu Flying Fox

MAMMALS OF THE SOUTHERN HEMISPHERE

Cheetah
Leopard
Jaguar
Spectacled Bear
Giant Otter
Amazon River
   Dolphin
Sperm Whale
Blue Whale
Humpback Whale
Proboscis Monkey
Chimpanzee
Mountain Gorilla
Orang-Utan
Ruffed Lemur
African Elephant
Black Rhinoceros
Giant Otter Shrew
Mulgara
Kangaroo Island
   Dunnart
Marsupial Mole
Koala
Long-beaked
   Echidna
Platypus

REPTILES AND AMPHIBIANS

Blunt-nosed
   Leopard Lizard
Pygmy Blue-
   tongued Skink
Komodo Dragon
Hawksbill Turtle
Yellow-blotched
   Sawback Map

Turtle
Galápagos Giant
   Tortoise
Jamaican Boa
Woma Python
Milos Viper
Chinese Alligator
American Crocodile
Gharial
Gila Monster
Japanese Giant
   Salamander
Olm
Mallorcan
   Midwife Toad
Golden Toad
Western Toad
Golden Mantella
Tomato Frog
Gastric-brooding
   Frog

GLOSSARY

adaptation Features of an animal that adjust it to its environment; may be produced by evolution—e.g., camouflage coloration

adaptive radiation Where a group of closely related animals (e.g., members of a family) have evolved differences from each other so that they can survive in different niches

amphibian Any cold-blooded vertebrate of the class Amphibia, typically living on land but breeding in the water; e.g., frogs, toads, newts, and salamanders

anterior The front part of an animal

arboreal Living in trees

bill The jaws of a bird, consisting of two bony mandibles, upper and lower, and their horny sheaths

biodiversity The variety of species and the variation within them

biome A major world landscape characterized by having similar plants and animals living in it, e.g., desert, rain forest, forest

blowhole The nostril opening on the head of a whale through which it breathes

breeding season The entire cycle of reproductive activity, from courtship, pair formation (and often establishment of territory) through nesting to independence of young

brood The young hatching from a single clutch of eggs

canine tooth A sharp stabbing tooth usually longer than the rest

carapace The upper part of a shell in a chelonian

carnivore An animal that eats other animals

carrion Rotting flesh of dead animals

cloaca Cavity in the pelvic region into which the alimentary canal, genital, and urinary ducts open

diurnal Active during the day

DNA (deoxyribonucleic acid) The substance that makes up the main part of the chromosomes of all living things; contains the genetic code that is handed down from generation to generation

dormancy A state in which—as a result of hormone action—growth is suspended and metabolic activity is reduced to a minimum

dorsal Relating to the back or spinal part of the body; usually the upper surface

echolocation The process of perception based on reaction to the pattern of reflected sound waves (echos); occurs in bats

ecology The study of plants and animals in relation to one another and to their surroundings

ecosystem A whole system in which plants, animals, and their environment interact

ectotherm Animal that relies on external heat sources to raise body temperature; also known as "cold-blooded"

endemic Found only in one geographical area, nowhere else

eutrophication an increase in the nutrient chemicals (nitrate, phosphate, etc.) in water, sometimes occurring naturally and sometimes caused by human activities, e.g., by the release of sewage or agricultural fertilizers

extinction Process of dying out at the end of which the very last individual dies, and the species is lost forever

feral Domestic animals that have gone wild and live independently of people

fluke Either of the two lobes of the tail of a whale or related animal; also a type of flatworm, usually parasitic

gene The basic unit of heredity, enabling one generation to pass on characteristics to its offspring

gestation The period of pregnancy in mammals, between fertilization of the egg and birth of the baby

herbivore An animal that eats plants (grazers and browsers are herbivores)

hibernation Becoming inactive in winter, with lowered body temperature to save energy. Hibernation takes place in a special nest or den called a hibernaculum

homeotherm An animal that can maintain a high and constant body temperature by means of internal processes; also called "warm-blooded"

inbreeding Breeding among closely related animals (e.g., cousins), leading to weakened genetic composition and reduced survival rates

incubation The act of keeping eggs warm for the period from laying the eggs to hatching

insectivore Animal that feeds on insects. Also used as a group name for hedgehogs, shrews, moles, etc.

keratin Tough, fibrous material that forms hair, feathers, nails, and protective plates on the skin of vertebrate animals

larva An immature form of an animal that develops into an adult form through metamorphosis

mammal Any animal of the class Mammalia—a warm-blooded vertebrate having mammary glands in the female that produce milk with which it nurses its young. The class includes bats, primates, rodents, and whales

metabolic rate The rate at which chemical activities occur within animals, including the exchange of gasses in respiration and the liberation of energy from food

metamorphosis The transformation of a larva into an adult

omnivore An animal that eats a wide range of both animal and vegetable food

parasite An animal or plant that lives on or within the body of another (the host) from which it obtains nourishment. The host is often harmed by the association

pheromone Scent produced by animals to enable others to find and recognize them

placenta The structure that links an embryo to its mother during pregnancy, allowing exchange of chemicals between them

posterior The hind end or behind another structure

quadruped Any animal that walks on four legs

raptor Bird with hooked bill and strong feet with sharp claws (talons) for seizing, killing, and dealing with prey; also known as birds of prey

reptile Any member of the class of cold-blooded vertebrates, Reptilia, including crocodiles, lizards, snakes, tortoises, turtles, and tuataras. Reptiles are characterized by an external covering of scales or horny plates. Most are egg-layers, but some give birth to live young

spawning The laying and fertilizing of eggs by fish and amphibians

vertebrate Animal with a backbone (e.g., fish, mammal, reptile), usually with skeleton made of bones, but sometimes softer cartilage

vertebrate Animal with a backbone (e.g., fish, mammal, reptile), usually with skeleton made of bones, but sometimes softer cartilage

FURTHER RESEARCH

Books

Mammals
Macdonald, David, *The New Encyclopedia of Mammals,* Oxford University Press, Oxford, U.K., 2009

Payne, Roger, *Among Whales*, Bantam Press, U.S., 1996

Reeves, R. R., and Leatherwood, S., *The Sierra Club Handbook of Whales and Dolphins of the World*, Sierra Club, U.S., 1988

Sherrow, Victoria, and Cohen, Sandee, *Endangered Mammals of North America*, Twenty-First Century Books, U.S., 1995

Whitaker, J. O., Audubon Society
Field Guide to North American Mammals, Alfred A. Knopf, New York, U.S., 1996

Wilson, Don E., and Mittermeier, Russell A., *Handbook of Mammals of the World Vol 1,* Lynx Edicions, Barcelona, Spain, 2009

Birds
Attenborough, David, *The Life of Birds,* BBC Books, London, U.K., 1998

BirdLife International, *State of the World's Birds: Indicators for our Changing World*, BirdLife International, Cambridge, U.K., 2008

del Hoyo, J., Elliott, A., and Sargatal, J., eds., *Handbook of Birds of the World Vols 1 to 15,* Lynx Edicions, Barcelona, Spain, 1992–2013

Dunn, Jon, and Alderfer, Jonathan K., *National Geographic Field Guide to the Birds of North America,* National Geographic Society, Washington D.C., U.S., 2006.

Harris, Tim, *Migration Hotspots of the World*, Bloomsbury/RSPB, London, U.K., 2013.

Stattersfield, A., Crosby, M., Long, A., and Wege, D., eds., *Endemic Bird Areas of the World: Priorities for Biodiversity Conservation*, BirdLife International, Cambridge, U.K., 1998

Fish
Buttfield, Helen, *The Secret Lives of Fishes*, Abrams, U.S., 2000

Dawes, John, and Campbell, Andrew, eds., *The New Encyclopedia of Aquatic Life, Facts On File*, New York, U.S., 2004

Reptiles and Amphibians
Corbett, Keith, *Conservation of European Reptiles and Amphibians,* Christopher Helm, London, U.K., 1989

Corton, Misty, *Leopard and Other South African Tortoises,* Carapace Press, London, U.K., 2000

Ernst, Carl H., and Lovich, Jeffrey E., *Turtles of the United States and Canada*. Johns Hopkins University Press, Baltimore, U.S., 2009.

Hofrichter, Robert, *Amphibians: The World of Frogs, Toads, Salamanders, and Newts*, Firefly Books, Canada, 2000

Stafford, Peter, *Snakes*, Natural History Museum, London, U.K., 2000

Taylor, Barbara, and O'Shea, Mark. *Great Big Book of Snakes and Reptiles*, Hermes House, London, 2006.

Insects
Eaton, Eric R. and Kaufman, Kenn. *Kaufman Field Guide to Insects of North America*, Houghton Mifflin, New York, U.S., 2007

Brock, Jim P., and Kaufman, Kenn. *Kaufman Field Guide to Butterflies of North America*, Houghton Mifflin, New York, U.S., 2006

General
Allaby, Michael, *A Dictionary of Ecology*, Oxford University Press, New York, U.S., 2010

Douglas, Dougal, and others, *Atlas of Life on Earth*, Barnes & Noble, New York, U.S., 2001

Web sites
www.nature.nps.gov United States National Park Service wildlife

www.abcbirds.org American Bird Conservancy. Articles, information about bird conservation in the Americas

www.birdlife.org The site of BirdLife International, highlighting projects to protect the populations of endangered species

www.cites.org CITES and IUCN listings. Search for animals by order, family, genus, species, or common name. Location by country and explanation of reasons for listings

www.cmc-ocean.org Facts, figures, and quizzes about marine life

www.darwinfoundation.org Charles Darwin Research Center

www.fauna-flora.org Information about animals and plants around the world on the site of the Flora and Fauna Conservation Society

www.earthsendangered.com
Information, links, books, and publications about rare and endangered species. Also includes information about conservation efforts and organizations

www.forests.org Includes forest conservation answers to queries

www.iucn.org Details of species, IUCN listings, and IUCN publications. Link to online Red Lists of threatened species at: www.iucnredlist.org

wwf.panda.org World Wide Fund for Nature (WWF). Newsroom, press releases, government reports, campaigns. Themed photogallery

www.wcs.org Wildlife Conservation Society site. Information on projects to help endangered animals in every continent.

wdcs.org Whale and Dolphin Conservation Society site. News, projects, and campaigns. Sightings database

INDEX

Words and page numbers in **bold type** indicate main references to the various topics.